FIERCE URGENCY

Education and Future Global Competition through Eyes of a Young Chinese Immigrant

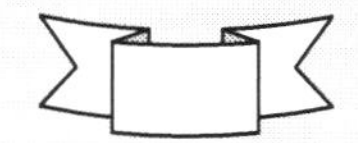

XIUZHE (WILLIAM) ZHAO

Cover design by Xiuzhe Zhao
Book design by Xiuzhe Zhao

Printed in the United States of America

First Printing: August 2009

ISBN-13 978-0-557-09107-2

CONTENTS

AUTHOR'S NOTE

Today, the prevalent topic of discussion in United States is China and the advent of intense global competition. Americans have the propensity to talk about the emergence of China as a dominant force in the world. They talk about how Chinese are stealing jobs away from Americans. They chat about the competitive edge of the Chinese in different aspects of the economy such as education, determination, and scientific ingenuity. Most importantly, Americans have been surprised by Chinese young people's work ethics and discipline, especially on the front of education. With those worries, many Americans are no longer sure if they can still remain competitive in this emerging global market and economy.

Nowadays, you can hear the discussions and see the fascinations of Americans over the success of the

Chinese in developing a group of strong and dedicated young people. These are the people who can potentially make China the most powerful nation in the world. No matter where you live or what channels you watch on television, you probably have seen and heard politicians using the growing competitive nature of Chinese to motivate American young people to work harder and to accomplish greater feats. I personally observed public officials such as the Governor, Treasurer, Secretary of State, and Superintendent of Public Instructions in Indiana talking about the increasing pressure of American students to compete with their counterparts in China and India. Many of you probably even heard incumbent President Barack Obama talking about the same issue. When the President of United States puts emphasis on an issue, it means the issue is serious, and we can no longer afford to ignore the topic any longer.

Nowadays, rhetoric is not enough for American young people to face the challenges ahead of them. Understanding that there is immense competition thousands of miles away will not motivate American young people to work harder. To them, the competition is simply too unreal and too far away to be significant and life-altering. Even if young Americans truly comprehend the critical nature of today's global competition and the desperate need to step up, they still do not know how to deal with challenge of this magnitude. China is simply too far away from here, and everything is still quite a mystery. If I were in the shoes of young Americans, I know for certain that I would not know what to do to face this challenge.

In order for American young people and the entire Western civilization to take on the challenge and face the competition, they need to truly understand the mentality and backgrounds behind the Chinese emergence. American young people need to realize why their Chinese counterparts are so much more driven, dedicated, and competitive in the status quo. Without knowing those facts, Americans are simply acting like a blind person trying to fly an airplane. There would be no specific directions and steps to reach the final destination. Inherently, nothing can be seen ahead.

This is why I am writing this book to analyze and to unlock the mystery and seemingly invisible factors behind the success of Chinese, especially young people. By learning about their mentality and the reasons leading them to the unique edge in the globalized world, Americans can not only understand more about China and its people through the eyes of a young Chinese immigrant, but also use such knowledge to successfully prepare them for the global competition.

Many of you must wonder what qualifies me to discuss this topic. I have to be honest. I am not a scholar or a social scientist. I do not have PhDs in human psychology or international studies. I was never a professor, and I am not a professor at the moment. I am simply a teenager who has not even finished high school yet. However, I have enough personal experience and observation in both China and North America to discuss the topic. I was originally born in China. I lived there for the majority of my life before I immigrated to Canada and United States. Throughout my life, I have moved from place to place in both China and North America. I have lived in different areas of the world. I had the opportunities to meet people from both half of the earth. The topic I am about to discuss is my life. I lived through it. I have been lucky enough to see both sides and explore the mentality of people on both ends. For that, I think I am more than qualified. I am bringing in a new perspective and a cross-cultural view on this fierce urgency in education and coming global competition.

As a young man, I used to be an everyday Chinese student. I carried many of their mentalities and experienced a lot like many of Chinese young people are going through today. Then I moved to North America and saw how North Americans differ from the Chinese. Throughout my six years in America and Canada, I have constantly done observations and comparisons between Chinese young people and American young people. Through my experience, I have observed situations and realities that can answer the question on the disparity between Americans and Chinese. I want to share my observations and experiences to the American audience.

I see today's global competition in the form of a chess game. The main competitors in this chess game are America and China. At this very moment, the chess game has already begun. As a matter of fact, the game has already begun many years ago when China finally entered the world stage. Right now, the game is still at a setup phase. Both China and America are setting up their pieces before any form of real attack or movement.

We are now at the dawn of the preparation phase in this chess game. There is a very interesting twist to the game. We are seeing two very different strategies from the opposing sides. The United States is playing it safe like a conventional chess player. He plays in a defensive manner, in which all the pieces are set up for the defense of the king. America has been the champ to the chess game for a while, and he wants to do anything he can to not lose.

With a different philosophy, China is a new challenger to the game of chess. He has something to prove. He is ravenous, and he wants to win. That's why he is playing aggressively and strategically. He is not playing to prevent losing, but he is playing to win. In the preparation phase, China has already set up the pieces strategically in order to attack the opposing king. He has already thought many steps ahead of the opponent.

At the dawn of the preparation phase, China is strategically ahead and is prepared to attack for the win. China has just recently completed his last move in the preparation phase, and now is the time for America's move. What will America do? Will America standstill and fall into the strategic setups of China? Or will America finally wake up and counter those moves already made? The answers to those questions is about to unveil in the upcoming years. It's still an uncertainty. But what is certain is that America needs to know the setups of China before countering those moves.

I hope you can enjoy this book. As an American, you have a duty to help America, the chess player, to make the best strategic move in the chess game. However, before anything can happen, you need to decipher and understand the moves China already laid down. That's why I am writing this book to guide you through this process and to unveil the mysteries of the Chinese mentality toward global competition. I wish that you can learn from the information in this book and be prepared for the future global competition involving China and many more emerging nations.

Active vs. Passive System

In today's world, we are sensing a new wave. This new wave is globalization. Sometimes, we feel like this is a déjà vu in human history. About 10,000 years ago, mankind experienced one of the greatest changes in human history, the Agricultural Revolution. The revolution brought in a new style of living on earth. People no longer needed to travel from place to place like nomads following the revolution. In late 18th century and early 19th century, another wave of transformation began with the Industrial Revolution. Through this revolution, people began to move from farms and rural areas into cities to work in factories along side of machines. Yet after all those years, we are at another cornerstone in human history with the coming of globalization. And of course, like all changes in life, this transformation has been making Americans quite anxious.

For many years, especially the past decades or so, America has been the center of the world civilization. This is the place where all the smartest and most successful people on earth work and live. This is also the hub where everyone in the world is dying to enjoy and savor. America has been the most powerful and prosperous nation in the world since the decline of the British Empire and European dominance. However, with globalization, Americans are standing on the other side of prosperity and are witnessing the swift progress made by people living half a world away, in China and in India. Much of that progress has been the products of young people living in those countries. They have been driven, determined, dedicated, and disciplined. Frankly, these positive characterizations for young people have long been forgotten and erased in the American society.

Today, the concerns of Americans do not rest upon the proficiency of such growth in China. The efficiency is the major concern. The success rate of creating intelligent and globally competitive young men and women has been extraordinarily high in China and other rising nations like India. This is especially true when compared to America where school dropout rates have been at an all-time high and student academic achievements have been at an all-time low. Now many Americans start to wonder if America's dominance in the world following emergence of globalization is going to remain. If the answer is "doubtful", what has America been doing wrong in educating young people and what has China been doing differently? To begin our quest in search of those answers, we need to point our attention to the greatest difference between America and China, the education systems and policies.

As a young man who lived the first ten years of his life in China and last seven years of his life in America, it's appropriate for me to say that I have a cross-cultural view to today's reality that many Americans do not have. Throughout my life, I have lived through the differences between America and China. I have seen both sides and have a great understanding of the path leading to the disparity between Chinese young people and American young people. Without any doubts in my mind, one of the greatest contributors is the education system, its policies, and its philosophies.

One area where the two education systems differ is the stage of development. In many ways, the Chinese education system is still new in its development process, and the effects of such development have been very conspicuous and obvious for all of us. However, unlike Chinese education system's rapid development, the American education system has already ended the general stage of growth and development. Consequently, its effects from those past developments have already expired and lost the "wow" factor in the past few decades.

In 1956, Americans saw a huge and a monumental change in their society. Because of America's triumph both militarily and economically during both World Wars, America then was on the rise as a world power. Under such prospering environments, the education system in America began its swift growth and development. In that time frame, over 50% of Americans became white-collar workers. In many ways, the statistic signified that over half of the total population was well educated. They were intellectuals who had extraordinary skills with white-collar, middle-class jobs. This statistic also showed that American education system in 1956 was at the height of its development.

Today, we are already living in a world over 53 years after such height in the development of American education system. Like all systems and successes, American education system has to experience the growth-and-bust cycle. While 50 years ago the education system was at a period of growth, this same education system has since stopped development and is on the path of decline. Since we are living at a period of time when American education system is on the decline, the education of young people is naturally on the decline as well.

Many of you probably are disagreeing with me when I mentioned the decline of American education system. Without any doubts, the best and most competitive universities and colleges are in the United States. Hundreds of American post-secondary institutions are better and higher ranked than the best colleges and universities in China. While those facts are true, American education system is on a decline mainly due to the elementary and secondary education sectors of the education system. While post-secondary institutions are excellent in America, the earlier stages of the education system such as elementary, middle, and high schools are simply not up-to-par to prepare many young Americans for post-secondary institutions.

Like American education system, the Chinese education system also needs to experience the growth-and-bust cycle. However, contrasting with American education system, the Chinese education system is at a growth and development stage today in the 21st century. In some ways, today's education system in China is a déjà vu and replica of the American education system in 1956. This growth in education system has been a direct effect of China's booming economy and surging international status today.

With growth and development, the effects of a new education system can be very visible. Like America in 1956, Chinese education system is increasing the percentage of educated individuals at an exponential rate. This change has also been greater in magnitude in China. Since the population of China is 1.33 billion, the effects of increasing intellectual percentage will be greater and more overwhelming. A 1% increase in the number of intellectuals in China can be an equivalent of 10-20% increase in the United States based on the total number of people. It does not take a rocket-scientist to realize this fact!

In addition to the disparity on stage of development, both education systems and their policies differ on priorities and focuses. In American education system, the priorities and focuses at school have not been very clear. In general, American middle schools and high schools promote an all-rounded curriculum filled with language, science, mathematics, arts, social studies, and physical education. To be quite honest, from my experience in this system of education, I found that there is no focus whatsoever on academic studies. As we all know, a lack of focus will make the young people's understandings of school subjects to be quite shallow. On many occasions, the diversity of subjects without any focus does not allow young people to have in-depth understanding of the academic concepts. This has been the reality of American education system.

Today, the approach Chinese education system has taken is very different from that of American education system. Of course, the results are different as well. In China, the education system's policies and the direction of the education department place a sole focus on scientific studies. Today in China, there is a common motto in schools and in universities. The motto is "scientific education prospers nation." The Chinese today have a vision. They believe that science will be the key to success in the future with globalization and stiffening of global competition. In the 21st century, the Chinese education system and the society in general consider scientific education as the Holy Grail to future national progress and success internationally.

As a result, students in China place more focus on scientific subjects such as chemistry, physics, computer science, and mathematics. This priority in the system allows young people in China to explore science in an in-depth manner. Unlike the shallowness of American education, Chinese education allows students to not only learn science, but also excel in science. In return, such academic curriculum and focus result in better preparation for future career and future international competition. And of course, the idea is quite visionary. Who can argue that science is not the future, especially when everything we do involves technologies and scientific concepts? Most people would have thought that it would take no time for Americans to catch on. Yet most Americans still haven't. At the very least, the American education system has not redirected its focus.

While China places focus on science due to its potential in the 21st century, the Chinese education system also aims at a very specific goal at the present time. Because today is a transformational period both for China and its education system, educators in China are advocating fundamental changes to the education system, its major policies, and its general philosophies. This fundamental change includes a common goal: "creating a new intellectual class in China."

Where did that goal come from? For sure, it did not come out of the thin air. As a matter of fact, this goal has been the goal of Chinese government and Chinese society for a very long time. Due to unfavorable social, political, and economic conditions, such goal was never fulfilled. Nowadays, as China emerges as a world power, the desires for making that goal come true have never been higher.

As we all aware, China is a communist nation, at least on paper. Therefore, the government and the people have a common ideal, a more socialistic ideal. For people who are unfamiliar with some of the goals of socialistic idealists, I will try my best to introduce them as I learned them through my Chinese education and past experiences with socialists in China. From their perspective, the main goal of a socialist society is to create a large intellectual class of people that can move the society forward. Especially with today's emerging market economy, Chinese people, education system, and the government all have a consensus. They want to create an intellectual class, which majorities of Chinese people can belong. Because of this ideal and this goal, Chinese education system has been trying very hard to make it come true through disciplined and rigorous style of education.

In America, there is no such goal. In general, Americans believe that education is used to shape a group of responsible citizens. They can then become useful members of society and make important decisions for government through elections. This type of goal is very broad and very open-ended. It does not require young people to be intellectuals and highly educated. They can become useful members of society in many different ways. Ultimately, this broad goal has not helped American education system to enforce more rigorous educational standards like China does. Because of a lack of rigorous educational standards, young people are generally free-spirits, and only they can control their futures. As we all know quite well, most of those young people have not made the right decisions for themselves.

In direct contrast with America, China is looking into the future with a clear goal. For the Chinese, they are trying to anticipate the future and make moves necessary to adapt to the trends of the future. Today, intelligent Chinese men and women who work in the education system and the government see a change in the soon future. This is a change from industrialization to automation. Even when I was living in China, there is a common perception. Chinese believe that 20th century was dominated by industries and machines, and 21st century will be dominated by information because of automation. Because of a future with automation and need for information, the Chinese education system sees the importance of education for young people. They take standards of schools and educators very seriously because they see the value of information through education in the future.

Surprisingly, the education system in China is not only used for preparing young people. Another goal of the education system is to educate the farmers and the workers. Chinese society wants to convert that group of people from doing the jobs of the past into doing the jobs of the future. Through this process, China is not only producing intelligent and competitive young people, but it is also recreating older generations making them ready for global competition. Because of this type of education, China is aiming toward modernization both technologically and educationally.

In the past years, China has, for a long time, seen the value of education and information in the future. During those passing years, the Chinese education system has already been working very hard to make Chinese adults and young people adapt to the future demands. America, however, has only recently caught on to this type of anticipation and prediction for the future. Unfortunately, the American education system has not been equipping young people with necessary tools to face a new future with new demands. From my observation, without an immediate change in mentality and actions, America's future in a globalized world can be quite bleak.

Furthermore, the gap between American and Chinese education system has continue to grow with educational philosophy. In America, the general philosophy in education is to create a group of responsible citizens who will contribute to the society. In this light, Americans tend to merge the ideal of equality with the philosophy of education. Through my experience in United States, I have found that the general population is not condescending or elitist. Americans, both young and old, generally like to see the positives in different people. From this type of propensities for equality, the education system is more tolerant of common customs and secular ideas.

In contrast, the Chinese education system contemptuously looks down upon common customs, banalities, and secular ideas. There are basically two hierarchies in China. One is a hierarchy of idealists and intellectuals, and another is a hierarchy of commoners. The Chinese society wants more young people to fall into the first hierarchy. Because of a disparity on traditional beliefs, the Chinese unlike Americans do not tolerate citizens to be average with common customs and secular ideas. The Chinese, in general, wants to raise young people carefully and prevent them from falling into the "traps" of banalities and secularism. In essence, the Chinese are inherently idealists and perfectionists. As those people, we all know that anything below extraordinary and ideal is a huge disappointment.

In the status quo, a main goal in China is to develop idealists instead of commoners with common customs. With such goal and such traditional philosophy, the education system has been defining and differentiating an idealist from a commoner through four main qualities: ambitious, moral, educated, and disciplined. Those who have those qualities are idealists, and those who don't are commoners. Quintessentially, the education system is educating young people toward achieving those four qualities and preventing them from falling into the "commoner" category. With the intention of achieving that goal, the Chinese education system has been taking drastic measures.

In order to produce idealists and perfectionists who are untainted from the society of common customs and secularism, the Chinese education system has ushered in a new philosophy on education. Unlike American education system, the Chinese system is trying to separate school system from the outside world. That is to say, the Chinese school system has deliberately segregated the young people and their schools from the society and its secular ideas.

In China, schools and education have been placed on top of a pedestal away from society. The education system under the leadership of the Chinese education ministers and educators has been characterized as a sanctuary. Education is supposedly an escape from the corruptions in society with all the common customs and banalities. To them, schools should act as a shield to disconnect young people from society and truly allow them to train in becoming idealists in the future. In some ways, it seems like that young people are being sequestered away from reality.

With the separation between education system and society, Chinese young people today have lost touch with the real society and its opportunities and options. This exact situation has shielded Chinese young people from the potential distractions that exist in society. They, under such separation, can truly place their whole focus on education and on the process of becoming idealists. With focus, they have gained a lot of in-depth knowledge in many areas, especially science. The in-depth understanding of scientific concepts has aided young Chinese to become experts in those scientific fields. In return, they become more competitive in global competition. This is especially true as our world today approaches to a more technological and scientific-driven world.

Although this kind of divide between education and society is quite odd to many Americans, this extreme measure and philosophy have seen many positive effects. Under the system, the Chinese have been able to train some very ambitious and high-quality young people who have fulfilled the standards as idealists. As the system originally predicted, this group of idealists uncorrupted by society's common customs and bad habits has been promoting rapid progress in China. This same progress has allowed China to rise as one of the world's greatest power with an overwhelmingly prosperous economy. In this same education system, educators have also been teaching the idea of "selfless contribution to society following education and success." Due to such instruction, Chinese young people have bought into the idea and implemented it through their continuous contributions to the Chinese society.

Under this more active Chinese education system, the educators and school systems have also been upholding the idea of accountability. Because the system is more active and more in control, the educators are naturally more accountable for the achievements of the young people. Instead of blaming the young people for not succeeding, the education system is taking those responsibilities and burdens.

In China, teachers have to also separate personal issues from their jobs and duties at school. On almost all occasions, the Chinese teachers, in the eyes of the students, are only educators, not friends to the students. When students lose interests in education and begin to decrease focus, the system will immediately make necessary adjustments and corrections. Teachers and parents are usually fulfilling the roles of correctors to young people. Sometimes, this includes drastic measures such as harsher punishments for young people at school.

In America, from my experience, I found that the teachers sometimes like to lay blame on the students for not focusing and not achieving academically. In return, the students place the burden on the educators to motivate them and to help them succeed. With this dynamic, American education system has not been able to make progress, and young people are starting to fail and to drop out of school. Additionally, the situation has been worsened as many American teachers combine personal feelings with jobs at school. Sometimes, they act like friends to the young people and create an unsuccessful and awkward dynamic for young people to focus and succeed.

Adhering to the philosophy of the Chinese education system, young people in China, in general, have to wear school uniforms. This idea has been quite universal in the country. The education system wants to promote a more austere lifestyle among young people. If they were not required to wear school uniforms, the young people would then dress individually like most American students. Under such circumstances, as many of you know, young people tend to compare and discuss their dress attires. Someone who lives in a wealthy family may then wear a designer jacket and brags about it. In the eyes of Chinese educators, those are unnecessary distractions preventing young people from focusing on education.

In similar manner, the Chinese education system has been very strict on the dress codes. Not only will most young Chinese wear school uniforms to school, they are not allowed to wear lipsticks and makeup. Although this is not completely implemented across schools in China at the very moment, this is the direction Chinese education system is going. With strict dress codes and policies, students will not be distracted from teenage dating, violence, and competitions outside of education. Unfortunately, since American education system is more passive, those rules are not in consideration. As a result, American young people are always trapped in this endless cycle of distractions.

Clearly, the Chinese education system differs greatly from American education system. This disparity allows Chinese educators to be more active and American educators to be more passive. As a result, we see a very clear and unsurprising reality. The Chinese young people, in general, are better prepared for global competition and future careers. They have in-depth knowledge in science and mathematics. Those can then lead to careers in very popular and demanding fields in the future. With fewer distractions from the secular world, they can really dig down and reach for those goals without distractions. In contrast, American young people are less prepared and are nevertheless anxious about the future as globalization and global competition pick up their pace.

As I look at the direction Americans and American education system is going, I can relate today's reality to the story of *The Odyssey*. For those who are unfamiliar to *The Odyssey*, here is the connection. In *The Odyssey*, a Greek hero Odysseus was lost at sea and he was trying to find a way home. During his famous voyage on the sea, he had to face many obstacles. One of such was the sweet singling nymphs. They were on an island at sea trying to lure Odysseus into their traps with their singings and beauties. In the end, Odysseus chose not to fall under that spell with the help of his sailors. Today, young Americans are like the Greek hero, Odysseus. They are lost at sea. As young Americans are trying to find their ways to success, there are many distractions. Those distractions are like the nymphs in the story. At this moment, we are passing by the island that holds all the nymphs and their traps. This is a decision time. Will young Americans fall into the traps of distractions? Or will young Americans act like the wise and sage Odysseus and walk away?

Impoverished vs. Wealthy

"The Chinese children are working so much harder than the American children! Why? What can I do to motivate my kids?" I have heard such comments simply too many times throughout my years living in America. I have heard them from teachers at school who were frustrated about American teenagers' lack of motivation to succeed and learn at school. I have heard them from parents who have high expectations for their children. I have even heard them from politicians both at a state and national level in the United States. Almost everyone in this country and Western Hemisphere in general is puzzled by the resolve and determination of Chinese youth. Many want to create a similar condition for their children to reach similar level of success in America. Unfortunately, the inherit conditions of China are the main contributors to such effects, and there are very little Americans can do to replicate such conditions.

I don't want to sound negative, but this is very true. America is simply too wealthy a nation to create a group of young adults who are hungry enough to do everything to succeed and to thrive. Throughout history, we have seen the struggles between the "haves" and the "have nots." Usually, the "have nots" work a lot harder to attain a certain goal. This same philosophy applies to the mentality of many Chinese teenagers today.

My family is a very typical family in China. Without a doubt, the journey my entire family went through demonstrates the mentality of many Chinese young adults today. In my opinion, my father is the epitome of someone with the mentality and behaviors of a "have not". When he was a kid, he lived in the northern region of China. Both his mother and father did not have the opportunities to attend higher education institutions. When my father's parents were young, China was still entrapped in decades of turmoil prior to the Communist Revolution. Even though the society, instead of their intelligence, had prevented my father's parents from a wealthy and comforting life, they had to suffer the consequences.

Because of the inherent conditions of my father's family, they lived in abject conditions in a rural area with four other siblings. The word "poverty" would not even be an exaggerated delineation of my father's youth. While many American children today take food and drinks for granted, my father as a child never did. Instead of imploring for iPods and X-Box 360 during holidays, all my father hoped for was a traditional Chinese meal that would last him for many days to come.

My father never enjoyed the luxury of bikes—not to mention modern transportations like cars and buses. Every day, he had to walk miles from his little farm house to his school. Of course, the Chinese education system did not offer school bus services like American schools. Schools still don't offer such service today. The entire education system is quite underprivileged compared to American education system. He walked through steamy summers and freezing winters without any complaints. Sometimes, I am simply in awe that he went through all those obstacles as a youth. When I think the way I live today, it's definitely incredible that my father suffered and survived through those times. I would not even walk home from school, and my school is only less than 10 minutes away from my house!

Many of you would wonder why. Why would he work so hard to go to a place as dreadful and dull as school? Why wouldn't he simply stay home and enjoy life like many of us today? The answer to the first question is simple. He had no choice. As a child living in an impoverished family, he understood his inescapable conditions at the time and developed a personal resolve to change such conditions in the future. He was an intelligent man, and he knew that there were people who lived in mansions and in houses full of luxuries. Since he never enjoyed those privileges, he as a normal human being with normal human mentality decided to do everything he could to reach the summit of wealth. For him, the only way for the pursuit of happiness and wealth was to go to school and college. Through higher level of education, he could alter his original status and become a member of the intellectual class in China. Those people were then assigned to respectable jobs in needed areas following graduation from college.

Like those people, my father who excelled in math and science majored in engineering and was assigned to a research and design institution in northern China following graduation as a PhD. His early hard work and dedication in education paid off. Because of his bachelor's degree, master's degree, and PhD degree, my father was able to become a professor in a respectable Chinese university later in life. The same accomplishments in education allowed my father to become an expert on engineering in China. His determination in the pursuit of higher education enabled him to live a good and fulfilling life in China. As a result of his early endeavors, my parents and I were able to have a more comfortable life.

Many of you probably think that my father's story is too antiquated and simply do not apply to today's societal conditions in China. Such assumption is valid, but it is incorrect. You may be surprised how many young Chinese today who are experiencing similar kind of poverties as my father did. This number is quite astounding due to the fact that China is still a developing nation. The gap between the wealthy and the poor is gigantic—much more serious than it is in the United States. Majority of Chinese still have below-par standard of living, and that's a lot of people. That's the majority of 1.33 billion people to be more specific.

Not only did my father had to suffer through a rough childhood as one of the "have nots", I did too. Of course, it was most likely not as terrible and harsh as my father's living conditions as a youth. In comparison to American children's childhoods, my childhood was simply below-average. I never enjoyed the standard of living many American children are enjoying today.

Today, many friends of mine in America are always puzzled when I attempt to do everything possible to succeed at school. The same friends also accepted it since I am Chinese. Yet after years of stereotyping on the mentality of Chinese teenagers, we still yet to find a sensible answer. Many Americans today still conceive that the dedication of Chinese students on school is the result of their parents' pressure at home. Although such assumption is not exactly wrong, it is not exactly right either. Without a doubt, my parents like many other Chinese students' parents like to pressure their children to study harder and to earn good grades. However, I, like many other Chinese students, do not see the pressure of our parents as the sole force behind our determination to succeed at school and in life.

When I was a child few years ago, I lived in China with my grandparents from my mother's side while my parents were trying to find jobs across the country. At that time, I lived in a small apartment building with my grandparents, my aunt, and my uncle. Every month, we had to live with the retirement funds of my grandfather, which was only $1500 in Chinese Yuan. Because it was only $1500 per month, we had to budget on what we buy and what we eat. I can still remember that I was limited to one McDonald's meal per month because of the tight budget. Since then, I realized that I needed to work hard at school in order to get into an elite college. It was only through the path of college I could become a member of the wealthy class. Then I can go out to eat at anytime.

To be quite clear, the grandfather who earned $1500 Yuan was an engineer similar to my father. This shows relatively how the Chinese are living a lower standard of life compared to Americans. My grandfather was one of the fortunate ones who had a great job. Yet he only earned $1500 Yuan during retirement. Additionally, a McDonald's meal was a delicacy in China. Having McDonald's once a month was actually a sign of great fortune. Many people at the time could not even afford to eat McDonald's at all. This reality directly proves that Americans are wealthier than the Chinese. Even one of the middle-class and educated engineers like my grandfather is considered to be poor in the United States.

Undoubtedly, the seed of determination was already planted in China, and it continued to grow in America. As a new immigrant in America, my determination not only remained, but also grew exponentially because of the new circumstances. Like many teenagers from an immigrant family, I knew that I needed to work hundreds of times harder than the indigenous American students. I saw myself standing in this country with a huge disadvantage because of my lack of understanding for the English language and the American culture.

I have to be completely honest. Even though many Americans today claim that opportunities are equal to everyone in America, I knew that those claims were untrue. I knew that I would not be taken seriously if I did not immediately have a grasp of the English language and the American culture. Due to the situation presented to me, I had to study countless hours a day to learn how to understand, speak, read, and write the English language. At school, kids used to tease me with profane English slangs. Since I did not know them, I was humiliated. The more American and Canadian children teased me the harder I studied the language.

From this experience at the beginning of my journey in a foreign nation, I already firmly established my determination and saw the challenge ahead of me. Although I realized that my intelligence and abilities could assist me in the future, I also saw myself as an outsider looking into a nation strange from my perspective. With my Chinese mentality, I continued to study and to prepare myself for global competition. As a Chinese boy, I inherently have to be humble because of my past conditions. Those conditions continued to push me to work harder and harder.

In addition to learning new culture, I encountered a new wave of poverty in North America. After my family first settled in Vancouver, Canada, we were facing tough challenges financially. While my mother was a successful educator in China, she could not find similar comfort in Canada. Initially, my mother applied for jobs related to her field, the field of education. Despite her years of expertise in the field of education, she was rejected countless times by major institutions because she was unable to communicate effectively during interviews. Her language barrier at the time was simply too great for her to acquire a career related white-collar job.

For a long time, my mother was a blue-collar laborer. My mother, in Canada, worked as an assembly worker in a curtain factory. On weekends, she also worked as a part-time cashier at a local fresh juice store like Jamba Juice. The combined net income for our family for a very long period of time was about $1500 per month. About $800 of the income was used to pay rent. After spending over half of the monthly income on rent, we were only able to manage to live in the basement of another family's house. It took us over one year to move out of the basement of another's house in Canada. It was a very difficult period for my family.

Those times were tough. I as a child never had the luxuries like many Canadian and American children. I can still vividly remember how my mouth watered when I saw food ads on television. All I could do was watch them. For me, food has always been a very important part of my life. When I was living in China, I always liked to go to restaurants. In Canada, we simply could not use the very little amount of money we had on restaurants and unnecessary luxuries. At that time, I could only resist my temptations. I felt so emotionally and mentally hungry that I became very determined to succeed at school and make a lot of money in the future.

During the holidays, many children from my school received gifts from their parents. They got Beyblades, Yu-gi-oh cards, video games, and many other cool toys. Unlike them, my mother and I had to go to a charity event at Vancouver's Chinatown. There, we saw many new immigrants and their children from China and many other developing countries. At this event, we, the children of immigrants, received gifts donated by the local community. Of course, I was happy that I could finally have some new toys. However, I was extremely concerned about the impoverished living condition. My determinations and resolve for success continued to grow like adding woods to a growing fire.

While I was enjoying the few new toys I received, I saw the eyes of many children there. I could see their determinations as well. I was not alone. Their determinations were similar to mine. We were tired of living as the lower class of society. We were tired that we could not have gifts during the holidays. We were tired that we could not enjoy restaurants that were so commonplace for the locals. We were tired to be treated as a second-class citizens and outsiders. At the time, we knew that the only way for us to reach the same playing field as the Canadians and Americans was to study hard at school and to attend an elite university where our talents can guide us into the upper society.

My father's and my experiences with below-par living conditions, to some extent, are simply two of many stories in developing nations like China and India. My stories are actually a lot more tolerable compare to many of those other stories. Fortunately, my story ended with a happy ending as my family emerged into the middle-class status in both China and United States. I have heard about children in China who are extremely poor. Many of their parents died prematurely, and they had to take care of younger siblings. I have also seen young people in China who not only had to dedicate hours to their education, but they also had to work in order to buy food for the family. I even saw young people in China who had to sale their organs in order to pay for food and their education at school.

Of course, those are some very extreme conditions, and not everyone in China traps in such dire conditions. When I mention the conditions of many Chinese, I am not trying to defame or slander the Chinese culture. I would never attempt to do so because I have always been a very proud member of the Chinese race. I take pride in my ethnicity, and all people who know me can justify this fact. However, I cannot deny the fact that a lot more people in China are living in a lower standard compared to Americans. As any developing nation, China is still not as wealthy as many developed countries in a general sense. While China has been making a lot of progress since its economic rise through reform, the country has not yet reached the level of the industrialized world.

Ironically, these relatively impoverished conditions are one of several reasons why teenagers in developing countries such as China are so much more competitive compared to American teenagers in general. Chinese students like my father at a young age are the "have nots", and they have experienced life in the lower level of society. In general, China's living standard is worse than that of America. Even the less wealthy groups of Americans are living in a higher standard compared to most Chinese and Indians when measuring with international living standards. Because Chinese young people have either lived through or seen impoverished conditions, they have become more mature and more prepared for global competition. With their past torments, they know that they need to work harder than other people in the world in order to succeed in the future.

I have to give a lot of credit to the Chinese. Throughout my life, I have been studying Chinese history and great leaders. With those studies, I have learned a very important fact. Although the Chinese have been the underdog and the disadvantaged throughout the timeline of world history, the Chinese has always been persevering, ambitious, and determined. For centuries, the nation, which many at the time had counted off, has been taking advantage of the "have not" conditions and used them as motivations to succeed and to work harder. Just like the spirit of the nation, young Chinese today are using the same mentalities to gear up for the global competition.

Nowadays, teenagers in China and India feel that Americans are simply too lucky with all the opportunities and luxuries. American children can go to school for free while Chinese children have to earn their ways into school. American children take cars for granted as a type of transportation while Chinese children have to walk from place to place (or take a bus as luxury). American children think an embarrassing birthday party as the greatest disaster in the world while many Chinese children have to earn enough money to even go to high school.

The differences in wealth and living standards have shaped two very different groups of young people. On one hand, we have today's youth in America. American teenagers, although they do not realize it, are the lucky ones. Even the poorest teenagers have the opportunity to find a job and to purchase food for survival. Even if the person does not have money, there are always charity organizations and churches that provide meals and accommodations.

American teenagers have every advantage that exists. They have the best post-secondary institutions in the world. They have the best standard of living. They have the best technologies. They have the best and most powerful country to live in. Sometimes, these advantages are taken for granted. Often such mentality leads to too much contentment.

On the other hand, we have teenagers from China and many other developing nations like India. They have always been the outsiders looking into the opportunities that exist in America. Most of them have lived in terrible situations and experienced poverty in some extent. Their conditions are simply intolerable compared to those of American teenagers. While they are looking in, they see how many American teens are throwing their opportunities away by dropping out of school and refusing to try harder. They also see how American schools are falling behind on education because of lack of efforts from students.

Because of their impoverished conditions, they are hungry, and they want to grab onto an opportunity every chance they get. In the status quo, they see a door opening because American students are throwing so many opportunities away due to lack of motivation and efforts. They feel that they can truly compete and win against their counterparts in America. That's why young people work a lot harder in countries like China and India. They know that their talent polished by education will allow them to challenge the "haves" or the American students. They are desperate to escape from poverty like my father and many other Chinese did. As someone who both saw and experienced such conditions, I know exactly how strong these feelings and determinations are.

THREE

Childhood Hardship vs. Happiness

After arriving in America, I made a great friend. His name is Matthew. In many ways, he is a great friend as well as a great competitor of mine at school. Like me, he places a lot of dedication and focus on school works and achievements. While we both do well academically and hold a great friendship, we can be no more different on work ethics and habits.

Matthew, in many ways, is an opposite of me. He is not very laid-back. When it comes to school, he really shows that he cares. Soon after knowing him, I took notice of his work ethics and habits. He is a person I bet many of you have dealt with and seen before at your own schools. Matthew is a guy with a go-getter spirit. Every time when the teacher assigns homework and projects, Matthew always goes home immediately and completes it as quickly as possible, long before the due dates. When I asked him why, he told me that he wants to get the assignments over with and be relaxed in the future as the due dates approach.

Although Matthew and I are friends, we cannot be any more different when it comes to completing assignments. I am someone you may label as a procrastinator. Unlike Matthew, I never consider the assignment until one or two days before the due date. That's when I usually start my project. My philosophy when it comes to homework and projects is to enjoy the days before the due dates and to suffer through hardship when the due dates approach. I am someone who lives in the present and worries only when it's absolutely necessary.

When I recall this disparity between Matthew and me, I begin to realize that this untypical and odd relationship actually applies to the relationship between China and America. Although China and America have always had a very good diplomatic relationship, the ways of life and mentalities on life cannot be any more different.

Throughout my life in America, I have always been asked about the work ethics and habits of Chinese young people. Nowadays, it's no longer a secret that Chinese people work a lot harder in education and many aspects of life in comparison to Americans. One big reason for this type of work ethics is the mentality they have. Chinese people today have mentalities similar to that of Matthew when dealing with school assignments. Chinese, in general, always think about the future and, consequently, are willing to exchange hardships at a young age in order to attain a great future.

During the years when I was living in China, I was a youngster. I had lived there since my birth and until ten years of age. At a young age, the society and my family introduced hardship into my life as soon as I entered kindergarten. Since I was six years old, my family had been trying to push a pile of works onto me. Before that age, I can say that I lived a pretty carefree life. All I did was play and sleep. But it quickly changed at the age of six following a great birthday.

I can remember the time when my parents were extremely furious when I could not add and subtract numbers while studying in kindergarten. They were so worried. They thought that I would become a failure and a lost cause in the future if I continued to play and enjoy life as a child. As a result, that was the day when I embarked on a life of hardship as a child through hours of studying. I never thought that would change until I heard that I was moving to North America when I was ten years old. That was the greatest moment of relief in my life.

While I was hard at work as a child, I acted like most children would do. I detested all the work and all the assignments I had. I wanted to give up, and I felt much betrayed. The only word I could use to describe the situation was "unfair." Of course, it was an equivalent of "unfair" in Chinese! But you probably get the idea.

On multiple occasions, I asked my parents why I had to suffer though such hardship. I told them that I was only a child, and it was unfair that I had to suffer so much at such a young age. To no avail, I received the same answer on all those attempts. At that age, I could not understand. I thought that the answer was absurd and stupid. I even threatened to run away from home because my parents were so forceful with my school works. But again, I was only around six years old!

Recently, I paid a visit to my memory lane and pondered over the answer my parents gave me. Now it makes more sense combining with my knowledge of the world. According to my memory, I remember that my parents told me that hardship in an early age was indispensably necessary. To them, experiencing hardship at a young age would make my later life as an adult happier and more fulfilling.

My parents were big believers in setting a great foundation, and they wanted to create a great foundation in my life at an early age. Then I could be self-sufficient later in life with my great foundation. They always used a metaphor to explain the concept to me. My mother, on many occasions, told me that a person's life is like a building. It requires a great foundation before construction workers can make the building taller. If a building were to build with a weak foundation, many levels can still be built above the ground. However, it will falter very quickly and very easily. My mother always thought that a person's life is like this building.

My parents also believed that having fun as a child would be a great risk and an incredible disadvantage in my life. They thought that if I were to throw my life away as a child by playing all day, my later life as an adult would be even more difficult and challenging. When that happens, the hardship would be even greater than the hardship of my childhood. In order to prevent that from happening, it was intelligent for me to work hard early for later success and comforts.

As I ponder over their answer, I begin to realize that this very idea does not only run around the minds of my parents. This same train of thought has jumped into the minds of almost all Chinese parents and educators today. We are at a point in history when difference between different cultures is inevitable. In this social circumstance, no one knows for sure why Americans and Chinese think differently on how a child should live. No one knows why Chinese people in an overall sense think childhood hardship is the key to happiness in the future. However, it is a reality, and it has affected the development of young people and the education system in those countries.

Half way across the globe, Americans do not agree with the Chinese philosophy on happiness and method for young people to live. If you are an American reading this book, I am pretty sure that you are frowning and disagreeing with Chinese educators and parents who place stress and hardship on young children.

In America, I found that the philosophy on a happy future is very different. In the first place, both Chinese and American cultures have a common goal. Both cultures hope to have young people who will live and lead happy lives as adults. However, the way to reach that place is very different. While Chinese parents and educators prefer hardship, Americans prefer childhood happiness.

In America, parents and educators don't think that having fun while young will corrupt the young people. They simply do not believe that having fun and playing at a young age are something dangerous. In direct contrast from the Chinese, many Americans I know think that not having fun as a child will actually make the child's adult life to be less happy. It's commonly believed that a bad and hard childhood will carry on and haunt a person's life forever. As a result of the carryover effect, the person will never be happy and will always live in the shadows of a disappointing past.

To Americans, a childhood is a once in a life opportunity. If it were to be damaged by hardship, there will be no more chance in the future to change that fact. Because of this type of thinking, American parents and educators really are open about children having fun all the time without stressing over work and burdens. To them, life is very long, and those young people will have plenty of time in the future to face those hardships. They don't need it now. In some ways, I feel that the

American mentality on this topic is very similar to my mentality with school assignments. If I have the opportunity to enjoy the present and deal with the hardship later, I will.

As a person who is fortunate to see both sides, I have to admit that I respect both type of mentality. For me, a culture needs to adopt what works the best for them. Just like school assignments, Matthew and I have very different approaches. In the end, nothing really matters when we both receive A's on those assignments. However, this is not really true today with the American approach.

Nowadays, we have seen a very sad reality. American young people are having too much fun, and the parents simply give them too much freedom for fun. Originally, I actually really enjoy the way Americans think about childhood and how it should consists of fun and freedom. However, today's situation is too extreme. The level of fun is just going over the tolerance level, and the excess has created many problems for young Americans.

Simply because of an innocent philosophy on having fun during a childhood, Americans are facing some severe consequences. Today, too many American parents and educators are too liberal. Due to the inherent philosophy, they allow young Americans to have fun. This fun has been heading toward an extreme. Many young Americans are taking advantage of the freedom for fun and completely throw their education away. I have seen too many great friends of mine in America who have thrown their lives and futures away by having too much fun. The worst part of it all is that those friends have so much potential and so much to offer to the world.

I have seen friends of mine who literally threw their lives away by having too much fun and driving incautiously. They are either heavily injured or deceased in the end. I have seen friends of mine who have skipped school on many occasions just to go have fun. In the end, they lose the opportunities to become educated and contribute to society. I have seen friends of mine who have committed crimes in order to enjoy a moment of thrill. In the end, they either go to prison or to a dead end in their lives. They lost their futures because criminal records will haunt them forever when they are trying to go to school or to find a job.

The reality of young Americans dropping out or throwing their lives away with unintelligent and vacuous actions is the direct result of a fun and carefree childhood. Maybe sometimes, the best option is the harshest option. This has to be our conclusion because the more lenient American option on educating children has failed. On the other hand, childhood hardship has helped the Chinese. I personally do not like this reality, but I know we all have to accept it.

FOUR

Social Tranquility vs. Struggle

When I first moved to America in ninth grade, I took a Physical Education class. Apparently, it is an Indiana requirement for a student to take a Physical Education class before attaining an honors diploma at graduation. Because I have always been terrible at sports, I did not like the requirement very much. This feeling continued as I attended the class.

Every day, I had to face a group of excessively energetic and rude American guys who simply could not control their hormones. This feeling of discontentment rose to an all time high when I witnessed some terrible actions many of the guys in class committed on the final exam day for Physical Education class.

During the finals, we were required to run one mile under a timed condition. In the end, the teacher would determine the grade based on the time we finished the run. I remember that day vividly because I dreaded that day for the longest period of time. I was just hoping to complete the run with a decent grade to pass. With my vivid memory of that day, I can still remember a classmate of mine, Jeff, and his reactions to the final exam.

That morning, Jeff was extremely nervous while we were changing in the locker room. I can still remember this because Jeff was never nervous in PE class. He had always been the best runner and the most athletic person in the class. To him, running a mile was a piece of cake. Before he runs, everyone knew that he had an A+ in his bag. That's why his nervousness was so noticeable.

Since he had always been a person who was good at sports but was never cocky about his abilities, I liked Jeff a lot as a friend. He was one of few nice guys in the class who actually have dignities and grace. Because of his great character, I went up to him and asked him what was wrong. As it turned out, he injured his ankle the morning before the final one mile run. He did not feel comfortable running that day, and he really was not confident about his performance.

I really felt his pain. I honestly felt really bad that someone like him had to deal with such an unfortunate event. But we could not do anything because it was the final exam, and there was no makeup for missing the run.

Like a warrior, Jeff took on the challenge that day. He actually tried his best to run the mile. Unfortunately, the pain was simply too great for him. Although he was running, his speed was not very fast. He was the last person to finish the run, and everyone in the class was shocked. To my surprise, many of the students in class actually made fun of Jeff for his performance. Although they already saw Jeff running with a limp and knew that he was injured, they were still ignorant and gave Jeff a very hard time. It was absolutely devastating to watch. What could Jeff do? He was handicapped that day.

Every time when I think about that incidence, I can relate that experience in a bigger way with today's world dynamic. Nowadays, many American educators and officials in education are placing the blames on the young people for not being as competitive and well-prepared as their counterparts in China and India. When I witness this situation, I begin to see those educators and officials as though they are the students in my PE class who laughed at Jeff's performance with ignorance.

With my observations, I have soon realized that the performance of many young Americans in education and preparation for global competition has been handicapped by the social struggles that exist in American society. Because of those issues' dramatic effects on young Americans, I personally believe that it's unfair for young people in America to take the blame.

One of the greatest social struggles in America is the problem with drugs and their connections to young people. America is inherently a very different country from China. It has been in the top of the world for a long period of time. The country has enough wealth for drugs to be a great problem among youth. Additionally, the liberal natures of the country and geographic locations have exacerbated the social dilemma.

More or less, America has been generally seen as a country that is quite liberal, especially in comparison to China. With this inherent nature, drugs would be more tolerable to the American society in some extent. The simple truth is that there are more opportunities for drugs to spread in America than in China. This inconvenient truth may offend many Americans, but we all know that it is absolutely accurate. Of course, the government and many sensible Americans are trying to fight against those drugs. However, the drugs have already immersed with the culture for too long for them to disappear forever.

Moreover, the geographic location of America does not really help the American social struggle with drugs. As we all know, drugs are mainly from Mexico, Latin America, and South America. And coincidently, the closest viable market for those drugs is America, which is right above South America and Latin America. As a matter fact, America and Mexico are neighbors. In many ways, drug problems in American society are quite inevitable if we look at the geographic setup and positioning.

With drugs being a great part of American society, young people are naturally the biggest predators to those drugs. Even at my school, which locates in a rural region of Indiana, has a great problem with young people using drugs. I have known several people—even the people I knew quite well—who got caught either possessing drugs on school property or using them. One of those people is a great friend named Ryan. We were classmates in a business class at school.

Since the beginning, I found Ryan to be a very intelligent and bright young man. I always thought that I was very gifted with school works. However I was proven wrong by Ryan on several occasions. In the business class, we were required to work on worksheets and find answers to many blanks. On multiple occasions, I was stumped by the question. Because Ryan was sitting beside me, he always helped me with those questions. That's when I found Ryan to be extremely brilliant.

The business class was a course during my freshman year. As I entered my sophomore year, Ryan became a senior. During a winter day in November, I remembered a huge fuss that occurred at my school. A group of police officers marched into the school building during lunch time, and they placed handcuffs around some guy. As people cleared up, I saw the guy's face. Initially, I could not believe that there was a criminal and a felon at my school. I initially was glad that I did not know a monster like that guy. As that guy turned around and walked into the police car, I was shocked. That guy was Ryan.

As the day went on, I talked to teachers and my fellow classmates. I wanted to know what happened to Ryan. He was so bright and so intelligent. I would never think in a million years that Ryan would be arrested, especially at such a young age. According to my teachers and classmates, Ryan was caught using drugs in the school's bathroom during lunch. When he was caught by a teacher, the teacher found more drugs in his backpack. I was simply flabbergasted. At the same time, I felt awful that a brilliant young man like Ryan destroyed his bright future with drugs.

Later that year, the school caught more students who were using drugs. Many of them were caught in the same situation in the bathrooms at school. Others were caught through random drug testing. The drug problem went out of control. The school had to remove all the doors in men's bathrooms at school. That was terrible. Now, many students at the school cannot even use the toilet because of a lack of doors.

I was hoping that the drug problem was only unique in my high school. Through personal research and readings from newspapers, I quickly found that young people's struggles with drugs were widespread, and they exist all over schools in America.

In contrast, on the other half of the globe, Chinese young people do not have the same struggle with drugs. Because of geographical limitations and severe measures taken by the education system, drugs are mainly free from most Chinese students. Even if young people could bypass those controls and censorships, they still cannot afford to purchase them. Drugs are usually the problem of the wealthy like Americans.

Despite the great effects of drugs on young Americans, drug among teenagers is not an isolated social struggle in America. There is also violence, both school and domestic violence. Such acts of violence have thrown young Americans off course from education and preparation for the future. It has been quite sad and unfortunate.

In American schools, violence is extremely common. It's almost too common. Under the freedom of choice and passive control from the education system, violence has taken a strong stand in American schools. Even at my high school, there are multiple acts of violence being conducted each week at lunch, even in the lunch room where teachers patrol. To young Americans, they have overused the powers they have in their hands and created a great social problem in American society.

In addition to poor choices, the access to guns and many other weapons have encouraged violence at school. Of course, I do not want to get into the controversial debate on gun possession. However, it's common sense that guns have increased the acts of violence in schools. At the least, the possession of weapons has given young people the options and the opportunities to hurt other people through violence.

Besides school violence, domestic violence has also played a major role in the lives of young Americans. No matter where we go, we will see people who have struggled with domestic violence. Even if you do not go to places, you can still find those instances on the news or on Oprah. In America, domestic violence is too common. Many families today are dealing with such acts of violence. As a result, the young people are traumatized mentally, and their performances at schools are usually affected as well to our expectation.

In my life, I have been fortunate to escape the tragedies of domestic violence. However, the safe environment within my home has not completely shielded me away from domestic violence. When I was in 8th grade, my family lived in an apartment complex. Because of our temporary condition, we did not rush into buying a house. While we were living there, I met a boy named Thomas. He was my neighbor in the apartment complex. We lived next door to each other. Quickly, we became friends. He was a fanatic of Yu-gi-oh cards, and I was too. We played and traded cards with each other on a daily basis.

When I met Thomas, it was during summer vacation. We had a fantastic summer together. Not only did we play Yu-gi-oh cards, he also showed me around the complex and the city since I was new to the area. To me, Thomas was this brilliant and funny guy who had a lot of dreams and a lot of heart. He was extremely nice to me, and I liked to hang out with him. As school began, I surprisingly found out that Thomas and I were in the same class together. I was thrilled!

As the school year continued, I began to see dramatic changes to the character and demeanors of Thomas. There were times when he became very violent and very threatening. It was not like he was going to hurt me. He simply acted violent with his incrementing temper. In the very beginning, I thought that he was just having a rough day or a rough week. However, his temper became worse and worse. With his temper, he developed a very bad attitude. He no longer wanted to listen to the teacher and always created problems in the classroom.

While everyone in the class was seeing a difference in Thomas, we all thought that the sudden change of character was extremely odd. Then one day, our teacher warned all of us in class that Thomas was diagnosed with some mental and emotional illness. Of course, he wasn't there when she told us that. Apparently, Thomas's family was experiencing a very rough time. His father continuously abused him and his mother mentally, verbally, and physically at home. Because of domestic violence, Thomas went through a lot of mental traumas. Those traumas later developed into mental illness, which led to his temper and his terrible attitude.

As I was listening closely to what the teacher was saying, I was shocked. For the first time in my life, I was exposed to the reality of domestic violence. For a long period of time, I thought that domestic violence was rare, and I would only witness it on the news. As a young adult, I simply could not believe that domestic violence took place right beside my apartment, and my dear friend Thomas was a victim. For some reason, I felt that I grew a lot that day as the teacher was warning us.

Through this experience, I finally realized that domestic violence is ubiquitous and omnipresent in America. It can affect almost anyone. When it reaches into the lives of teenagers, their lives are forever altered. When American young people are exposed to domestic violence, they often experience mental and emotional traumas. In return, they lose focus from their future and their education. Of course, those young people are victims. They should not be blamed. However, the effects are very real, and a lack of change to correct domestic violence in America will continue to haunt young Americans in the future.

In contrast to America, both school and domestic violence are not very common in China. At the very least, they are not as common as they are in America. In China, there is simply no option for choosing school and domestic violence. There is a zero tolerance for such behaviors, and the punishments are simply too severe for the Chinese to risk those actions. Additionally, the Chinese culture has historically been very conservative and disciplined. People who commit school or domestic violence are always heavily condemned and ostracized by the society. At school, the teachers who see potential participants of school violence will immediately utilize necessary procedures to prevent the event from occurring. It has been very effective.

Because of the degree of social struggles, young Americans are living in an environment full of corruptions and distractions. This environment truly tests their abilities and their strengths as individuals. Unfortunately, these struggles also prevent many young Americans from pursuing their dreams and fulfilling their duties in education. Many people due to those struggles have to drop out. In the end, not many young Americans can make all the way through. That has been a great problem in American education system. I truly hope that change is on the way before it is too late.

FIVE

Intense vs. Moderate Competition

It was July 3rd, 2009. I went out with one of my American friends, Jack. We went to a little restaurant called Olive Garden. Since we had not hanged out with each other for a while due to my trip to California, we had a great conversation. While we were dining at this Italian restaurant, we began to talk about each other's summer and plans for the remaining weeks during the break. We caught up with a lot of our exciting trips and activities.

During our casual chat, a light bulb lighted up in my mind. I thought that it would be a great idea if I could see the American perspective on Chinese young people and their accomplishments academically. I brought up that I was working on a book. I informed Jack that I wanted to explain why Chinese young people are generally ahead of Americans academically and in career preparation. Additionally, I told him that I wanted to write the book from my own perspective as a former Chinese teenager living in the United States. This way, my rich experiences and observations can really help Americans today who are anxious and nervous about the Chinese surge, especially among young people.

Similar to my expectations, he was interested in the topic. As a matter of fact, he personally was hoping to find some answers to this Chinese phenomenon as well. As an aspiring business major in college, Jack told me that he was anxious about competitions coming from China. With his interests in my endeavor, Jack gladly offered some opinions on the issue. Of course, I was dying to hear what an American high school student think about this topic.

To my surprise, he actually admitted that Chinese young people excel academically compared to American students including him. I never expected a great student like him to ever contain his ego and admit to this fact. From our conversation, I quickly learned what he believes.

He knew that Chinese students work a lot harder on education. In other words, they study a lot more than American students do. When I asked him to think about some possible reasons for this reality, he offered a very interesting perspective. He claimed that Chinese students have to really focus on education and career goals because they have no choice. They are facing a lot of competition within the country. He as an American teenager, however, does not have as many competitions as Chinese young men and women. From his point of view, Chinese young people would not have jobs and sources of livelihood if they do not work hard academically at school.

Of course, as a person who used to live in China as a young boy, I knew exactly what my American friend Jack was talking about. As a realist, I understood that there were a lot more reasons other than competition within a pool of large population. However, I have to admit that my friend was completely right. Sometimes, we tend to over think and over analyze an interesting phenomenon. We forget the obvious, and the obvious in this situation is the population factor in China.

Here are some very fascinating and extremely distinct statistics. Today, the United States has 304 million people. On the contrary, China has 1.33 billion people. For people who are not familiar with the word "billion", 1.33 billion people equal 1330 million people. China has over a billion (1000 million) more people than the United States has. Those simple statistics clearly explain why Chinese young people have to work harder and somehow excel in what they do.

Sure, Americans are concerned and skeptical about the future because Chinese people are getting increasingly competitive and are threatening the future lifestyles of many young Americans. They have the potential to take over traditionally American jobs. However, this new surge should never been a huge surprise. The population statistics speak for themselves. With the population in China, we should have already seen it coming.

Because of the large population, Chinese young people are not thinking about competing against Americans or Europeans. They have too much competition on their hands internally. In China, the reality is very simple and, quite frankly, very harsh. This reality is no stranger to us all. It's Social Darwinism.

Today, Social Darwinism, as it was proposed over a century ago by Herbert Spencer and Andrew Carnegie, is the idea of "the survival of the fittest". It was adapted from Darwin's theory of natural selection. In his theory, Darwin hypothesized that the speciation of organisms is the result of competition between individual organisms for limited resources. In Social Darwinism, however, it metaphorically interprets natural selection in social circumstances. For example, the individual organisms are human beings, and the limited resources are jobs and college acceptances instead of food.

In all honesty, Social Darwinism is universal. It exists in all areas of the world, and all citizens of the world have to deal with its harsh reality. But the degree and intensity of Social Darwinism differs from region to region. Ultimately, the main determinant to its degree and intensity is population, the number of people competing for those limited resources.

In our context, Americans have competitions as well, and for those living in the American society, it would be amusing to think competitions in the United States are nonexistent or weak. I, for sure, would not make such absurd assertions. But reality is reality. In comparison to China, United States does not have a very intense competition. Young Americans are not facing nearly as big a challenge in school as their Chinese counterparts do. And this is mainly caused by the differentiation in population.

In China today, the number of jobs and companies available are relatively similar to that of America. Of course, because of the size of China population-wise, it ought to have a little more job opportunities and companies. Nevertheless, the proportionality of the number of jobs to the total population is what really matters. Mathematically, the best way to compare opportunities available between China and United States is by dividing the total number of jobs/companies by the total population. I can almost guarantee that the result will be very different. The number for China will be very small, and the number for the United States will be relatively larger.

For those who are not good at math, I will explain it literally. Unlike America, however, the number of people competing for those jobs and companies in China are a lot more. To be more specific, over ONE BILLION people more. So the idea is simple. Metaphorically, not everyone is going to get a piece of pie in China while there are leftovers in America. I like this metaphor because it sums up the intensity of competition in China compared to that of America.

The escalating population and competition intensity have huge effects on the demeanors of Chinese young people. The reality of competition in China today forces young people to be more dedicated on education and on a specific major such as chemistry, engineering, physics, technology, computer science, and many more. They know that they need to not only do well academically in order to enter a university, but also excel in a specific field in order to acquire a job after graduation. I know this feeling very well because I used to be one of them.

While American young people are living the dream and enjoying life as teenagers, young Chinese are facing harsh realities. In many ways, I see American young people as Peter Pan. They do not want to grow up quickly, and they do not need to do so under such a comforting and relaxed environment. On the contrary, I see Chinese young people living in a wild jungle. Of course, they do not want to grow up quickly and want to enjoy the carefree life as teenagers. However, the circumstance of a jungle does not allow that. In the jungle-like environment in China, those who do not wake up and face reality will be eaten or destroyed. Those who do not follow an austere path for education will not survive. If they give up for one day on education, they would have to jeopardize their entire future.

If you think competitions for jobs in America is intense, just imagine yourself in China. This is no laughing matter. Because of the population difference, it's four times as hard for Chinese to find jobs as for Americans statistically. This reality forces Chinese students to go the extra miles in order to be more competitive. That's why Chinese students have to spend less time on leisure and more time on education.

Education is the safest way for young Chinese to achieve success. Academic achievement is a measurement of how competitive a person is in the Chinese society. Of course, academic achievement is like everything in life. It takes practice and time. Because Chinese young people have to face more competitions, they spend more time on academic works. The extra efforts make them better prepared and equipped than Americans of the same age. It's not because Chinese young people are smarter. It's simply that they work harder to adapt for the competition.

Exactly how hard? It's harder than many of you may think. In China, not to mention competitions for jobs, the competition for getting into a higher education institution is overwhelming. Here are some statistics on higher education.

In China, there are roughly a total of 2000 higher education institutions. Among those institutions, there are 6 million students in attendance. And remember that the total population of China is 1.33 billion. On the contrary, United States only has 304 million people. However, the country currently holds 5758 higher education institutions, and over 14 million students attend those institutions. In other words, the American students have much higher odds of getting into a college than Chinese students.

To be more specific, I did a simple numerical calculation from the statistics. My result indicates that 0.45% of the Chinese population attends college or university (hypothetically since not every one of 1.33

billion people is a student). In a similar calculation, I found that 4.6% of US population attends college or university (also hypothetically using the entire population). Young Americans have a ten times higher chance of getting accepted by a higher education institution than their Chinese counterparts have.

This reality directly reflects the intensity of competition in China among Chinese young people. When I was living there, I realized that everyone had great intensities toward education. They all know that competitions are fierce and that they need to step up their games in order to win.

On the contrary, this is not the mentality for American students. As a matter of fact, most American students are able to attend a higher education institution. Even if one flunks high school, he or she can still have an opportunity to attend a community college. On many occasions, the only reason for an American teenager to not attend a higher education institution is personal choice and personal priorities. On the other side of the globe, Chinese young people can only dream of such opportunities and such odds for themselves.

Now, you may wonder how does competition raises the competitive edge of Chinese young people in regard to global competition. The idea is very straightforward. Because Chinese young people face more competitions throughout their lives, they become more competitive and more refined as individuals. Usually, the brightest and the best of those 1.3 billion people become competitors on the world stage. In other words, the selection process is very tough in China, and the results are usually superior compared to other countries.

Nowadays, Americans have many opportunities and options. High percentages of students in America get accepted in college. Because of the lesser competition young Americans have to face, the results are not usually as competitive as the Chinese. The selection process (the competition itself) is not very rigorous, thus the students who end up competing internationally with the Chinese students have not been tested enough like their Chinese counterparts have.

In some ways, this type of situation reminds me of my experience in Future Business Leaders of America. Future Business Leaders of America is a student business organization dedicated to the education of students in business.

Every year, there is a state competition and a national competition in different business events such as Business Calculation, Accounting, Entrepreneurship, and Marketing. Since I live in Indiana, I always compete during the Indiana FBLA Conference every March. Through my experience in FBLA, I learned about how initial intensity of competition raises the overall competitive nature of the students.

Indiana is one of the smaller states in the country. Therefore there are less young people competing in those events during state competition. Because of the relatively easier competition, the selection process to qualify for nationals is not as rigorous as some larger states.

Unlike Indiana, California is the biggest state in America, and there are a lot of young people competing to represent California FBLA at nationals. Because the number of people competing on the state level, only a few percent of those students can represent the state, and obviously the selection process becomes very rigorous. Internally, California has to cut a lot of students before finding their candidates to compete for nationals. In the end of the selection process, the state usually finds the brightest and most competitive candidates.

After the selections of the states in the early spring, the states bring their best competitors in different business events to nationals. At nationals, those students from different states have to compete against one another. Of course, this means that the students from Indiana have to compete against students from California.

Due to the difference in intensity and standards during the state selection process, national qualifiers from California have dramatic edges over national qualifiers from Indiana. Honestly, they are stronger competitors compared to their Indiana counterparts in each business events. I even have to admit this, though I myself am from Indiana and was one of the qualifiers from Indiana.

For years, I have been trying to figure out why competitors from California are so GOOD! They win in so many events that I sometimes feel dumb as a competitor myself. As time went by, I began to realize why. The truth is that Californian competitors at nationals are narrowed down from thousands of students in California. Unlike them, Indiana competitors at nationals are selected from a pool of a hundreds of students. Of course, California wins more! They can find better candidates/competitors from such a huge group of people. Even though that was a reasonable result, I still feel bitter about California dominating the competition. This uneven playing field allowed California FBLA to win over 20 business events at nationals last year. On the other hand, Indiana FBLA had a goose egg on winning first place at nationals. The best result we had was a second place, and that was the best outcome for Indiana FBLA in years!

In many ways, I find that the FBLA system is a miniature model of today's international competition. Americans are worried that the Chinese are beginning to challenge and take over originally American jobs and major fields of work. However, there should not be this much surprise.

As we have seen from my FBLA experience, the competitive edges are developed internally on the local level. Before FBLA competitors reach nationals, the overall results were already shaped and determined. In similar manner, the competitive nature of Chinese is being shaped within China. Because of the intense competitions and the overwhelming number of competitors within China, the Chinese who finally succeed in specific fields are always the best of 1.33 billion people.

China, in this example, is California FBLA. My FBLA group, the Indiana Future Business Leaders of America, is the United States. The ones in the United States who succeed and challenge the Chinese for jobs on the international stage are selected from a pool of 304 million people. It's still tough competition, but the intensity and rigorous nature of such competition is far less than that from China. Therefore, the United States is Indiana FBLA in this situation. Since those Chinese are more refined and more tested, they have more edges facing their fellow American competitors. Moreover, the young Chinese are more educated and more disciplined. They were tested again and again in China. If they continue to achieve today, they have become very tough and very well trained for global competition. This reality usually results in the United States falling on the short end of the stick.

Unfortunately, this result is inevitable. There are no ways for Americans to fabricate a similar type of competition. However, there is still a slight piece of hope for young Americans today. Sure, the Chinese are inherently given better odds in international competition because of the nature of Chinese competition internally.

However, this odd can still be changed by Americans. While competition is a great way to train someone and refine someone for the future and the global competition, countries with fewer competitions like the United States can still have a light of hope.

Competition internally is a great determinant for international success. However, it's not the only factor in the mix. When I was telling my story about FBLA competitions between Indiana and California, I left out one part of the story. Sure, California FBLA crushed Indiana FBLA in competitions when we counted the overall awards won. However, Indiana did have a second place finisher on the national level. As a matter of fact, the person who created history for Indiana FBLA is a great friend of mine. His name is Jacob.

Jacob not only won second place in competition for Indiana FBLA at one national, but he has also consistently won competitions throughout the years at the state level in different events. Therefore it was not a stroke of luck. In order to compete with students from other states such as California, Jacob developed a unique yet effective mentality. He was not myopic and narrow in his perspective. He clearly knew and understood that winning at Indiana state competition was not enough to make him competitive nationally. With that mentality and belief, he ended up as a winner.

When he scored 80/100 at the Business Calculation competition in Indiana, he easily won. I mean he blew the competition out of the water! The second highest score was, as I recall, 58/100. However, he was not satisfied. He had a farsighted perspective and strong desires to succeed at national competition. Although 80/100 was enough for him blow pass the competitors in Indiana, he knew that such score was not enough to allow him to win nationally.

His national perspective and insight drove him to practice harder and to aim at a higher score. According to his prediction, he needed at least 98/100 on the Business Calculation test in order to have a chance to win at national competition facing competitors from states like California. His dissatisfaction with his score at state competition inspired and challenged him to work even harder in preparation.

I can still remember rooming with Jacob in the same hotel room at national competition. It was in Anaheim, California. When I called him two weeks prior to nationals, he told me he was studying for Business Calculation. I would have been shocked by his dedication. However, I knew him very well and expected him to work extremely hard to achieve his goals.

When we were there, everyone was enjoying the time in the big city in California—everyone except for Jacob. They were exploring the city. They were planning trips to Hollywood, Beverly Hills, and Disneyland. The boys were trying to hang out with girls from other states, and the girls were trying to have fun with "cute" boys from other states as well. Shamefully, I was one of those people who were confident about our results at state competition and thought we would just have fun in California instead of studying. On the contrary, Jacob had one goal in mind, winning at national competition.

When everyone was having fun, all Jacob did was staying in the hotel room and studying with his textbooks and practice tests. When everyone was out for dinner, Jacob only had bagels because he needed to study harder in order to win and did not want to waste time by going out for dinner. His tenacity was inspiring. As a result, he received second place at the national competition and helped Indiana FBLA in doing so. Winning second was huge for Indiana. For decades, the state did not have anyone place that high at nationals.

The main reason he won was that he saw the size of the hill he needed to climb facing intense competition from states like California, and he used hard work and dedication to conquer that hill. The idea is that simple! Yet it's so hard for so many people to go above and beyond to achieve!

Most Americans today do not have the Jacob Mentality. To be quite honest, I personally am like most Americans and do not have the Jacob Mentality. I am working on it! It truly takes a lot of determination and discipline to master such mentality and work ethics.

Americans, especially young Americans, do not see far enough. They only see competitions around them at school and in the class room. They only see competitions within the state and at the workplaces. They only see competitions in the United States and around its borders. They do not see competitions internationally in countries like China and India. This type of narrow thinking has been the downfall of many Americans, and it can be detrimental to the American society in the future.

The problem is not the competition in China that results in high quality individuals. Americans have no control over that. The problem is that Americans don't think and act with the Jacob Mentality. They get satisfied with their accomplishments nationally like most Indiana FBLA qualifiers. They don't see the competitions from China and India, and they therefore don't work harder to be competitive against individuals from those countries. On the other hand, the Chinese and the Indians not only have competition within their countries, but they also see competitions across the globe such as American competitions.

This reality and general mentality today have been hurting Americans more and more. I think it's time for Americans to finally wake up. Americans don't have the inherent advantage of a large pool of competitions. However, if all Americans act like my friend Jacob and carry the mentality that one needs to work harder in order to be competitive internationally, Americans will be in great shape. But because of the unawareness of competitions internationally as well as the destructive side of satisfaction and overconfidence, many young Americans have placed a shadow on their potentials. This is also partly the reason I am writing this book. I want to show Americans the competitions across the globe. I want people to know that the competitions are very real, and there is a fierce urgency for Americans to take action facing those challenges.

My best advice is called the Jacob Mentality. Americans need to truly see the competitive nature and advantages of their competitions internationally in China and in other countries. By understanding the reality, they can begin to get inspired and to work harder in order to compete. If this is the American mentality in the future, the United States will be in a great shape for the coming years.

To end this section, I want to metaphorically describe the challenges and mistakes many young Americans are making today. In some sense, many talented young Americans are medium-sized fishes. However, they live in a small pond. The pond is so small that the medium-sized fishes look gigantic in it. In a lake on the other side of the pond, there are large fishes that represent the young Chinese. Because of intense competition, they grew into large fishes. Although they are large fishes, the lake is still quite huge. Therefore, they don't really think they are really big and powerful. On the other hand, the medium fishes in the small pond think they are huge and powerful. When both types of fishes are placed in the ocean, which is a metaphor for the international stage, the medium fishes are too overconfident and think they will dominate the ocean as well. When they see the large fishes from the lake, they will be shocked. Eventually, the medium-sized fishes will be consumed by the large, refined, and modest large fishes from the lake. Is the fate of the medium fishes from the pond what we want for young Americans in the future?

Early Unemployment vs. Workaholic

What is the most stressful task in the world? The answer to this question is almost universal. It's a job. If you have ever lived in my family, this is definitely true, and you will know about it. Every day, my mother comes home and complains. She talks about how difficult her job is. Sometimes, she even threatens to quit her job because she feels overwhelmed with the hours she has to work. I can sense that she wants to retire early.

When my mother used to work for the company that manufactures Blackberry cell phones, she did the same thing. She complained about all the works she had to do with her job. Her job required her to work at nights. Such work schedule interfered with her daily routines. Throughout my life, I have lived in an atmosphere where jobs have been labeled as extremely stressful and pressure-driven. Sometimes, I feel fortunate because I do not have an official job as a teenager. However, not all American students have the same luxuries.

Most American friends of mine have jobs as high school students. To be quite honest, I would find a job as well if my parents did not forbid me from doing so. As a student, I want a job for two reasons. First and foremost, it's obviously money. As a teenager myself, I understand the mentalities of American students. For young people, the first step for personal freedom is a job. With the money earned from the job, we as teenagers can purchase whatever we want. If we want to have the new gaming system, we can then use our income to purchase it. If we want to buy a new pair of designer shoes, we can use our income as well. All those would not be possible if we solely rely on our parents. As we all know, parents usually would reject such proposals on normal occasions.

In addition to money, jobs have also emerged as an important aspect of American culture. Almost every American has worked as a teenager. Their friends work as high school students. Their parents most likely had worked as teenagers as well when they were young. In some ways, working as a student has been a great American tradition.

It's commonly believed in America that a job is a great opportunity to shape a young person's life. And I agree. It provides young people with the opportunity to see the real world at a young age. Additionally, they as young people can also experience the hardships their parents have to go through every day as employees of various companies or as self-employees. This experience can truly increase the appreciations among young people for their parents' hard works and dedications. Additionally, young people can quickly mature from such a fulfilling experience.

Although hardship coming from a job is a great way to shape character, it can also be negative. For one, it has definitely affected the focus and dedications of

American students on education such as academic achievements and school assignments. Usually, two outcomes occur when an American high school student has a job while still attending school. Such outcomes are almost too predictable. Yet many people still don't see jobs as threats to young people's education.

The first outcome is excessive stress. Because of all the extra hours on the job out of school, students with those jobs are most definitely drained. I know I will, and I think I am in pretty good shape! Young Americans may be too stressed to focus on school works because of the hours of the job. Although the lack of focus on school due to a job is understandable, it's absolutely unacceptable, especially for students who want to challenge the Chinese students on the other side of the globe. For me, this reality is no stranger.

I have a friend named Jason. We went to the same high school, and he was a grade higher than I was. I met him when we were taking a computer science course together. Although we soon became good friends, I knew that he was a mess when I first saw him.

Initially, I was puzzled. In class, he was a very talented computer programmer. While we were doing computer programming, Jason was simply brilliant. He had all the algorithms written down in his mind, and he usually finished all the assignments before other students could finish one assignment. From my perspective, he had to be one of the smartest students at school. Usually, a great programmer and computer science student requires outstanding mathematics skills, reasoning abilities, and a brilliant mind. Since Jason excelled in computer programming, he had to be tremendously talented with all those criteria. With his brilliance, I would never be surprised if he were the valedictorian of his class. However, I was greatly mistaken.

As I got to know him, we became great friends in the class. He was quite mischievous. Despite my friendship with Jason, in some ways, I found that he was a troubled student. He had a terrible temper. He criticized and yelled at the teacher on numerous occasions. Because of his brilliance in computer science, the teacher often allowed him to express his anger.

Eventually, I saw a pattern to his troubled demeanors in class and with the teacher. He was quite exotic with his patterns. Someday, he was great, and someday he was not. Soon, I saw a consistent pattern to his bad days. During those days, I quickly realized that he was always tired. Due to his fatigue, he not only created unnecessary anger, but he also slacked off on school works. His work ethics in the computer science class told me everything about him.

With his brilliance, he always succeeded on formal assessments and programming tests. However, his success was solely based on his brilliance. He never studied for the tests and the assessments. In class, he rarely listened to the teacher. His downfall at school was his lack of dedication on school works. When my computer science teacher handed out homework and in-class assignments, the brilliant Jason never even took a look at them. He simply threw them on the side and put his head down to sleep in class.

Obviously, homework and in-class assignments are great portions to the final grade in class. Although Jason aced all the tests and assessments, he finished the course with a low B. If he applied himself in class, I would never be surprised if he got an A+ in the course.

In the beginning, I thought that computer science was the only course, which he did not put a lot of efforts into due to his innate talents with programming. But I was wrong. I remembered one day when he was checking his grades on the internet. He offered me an opportunity to look at his grades in all his courses so he could complain about the teachers. When I was looking at his grades, I was simply stunned. He had B's, C's, and D's in his classes. The reason for his low grades was not that he failed tests or formal assessments. He received 0's in a lot of the homework assignments and in-class assignments. For me at the time, I was outright flabbergasted. If I were to have a brilliant mind like he has, I would never in a million year allow my grades to be that low due to lack of efforts. Eventually, I realized why.

So why did he get 0's on his assignments? I asked the exact same question after seeing his grades. The answer he gave me was straight forward. He told me that he had to work after school and during school nights. After working, he was too tired to work on homework assignments. Sometimes, he worked so hard on his job that he could not even stay awake at school.

I was very curious. I asked him why he was sleeping all the time at school. As an honest person, Jason told me. Ever since he got his job at a local restaurant, he found that school was not as important anymore. With the money he earned, he was quite satisfied as a teenager. Additionally, he had to sleep during class because he wanted to get ready for hours of work after school.

In some ways, his priorities changed with his job. Instead of focusing on school and seeing it as a valuable experience of his life, he put his job as a higher priority. Of course, such mentality is quite normal. As a teenager myself, I can understand that I sometimes think for the short term instead of long term. Working and earning money from the job are short term luxuries, and many young Americans are willing to give up the long term investment in education for short term gains. Because majority of American students do work, this same mentality and same altering priority have dramatically caused the decline in American education. This same reason allowed many young Chinese to surpass young Americans in education and competitive edge on the global market.

In addition to the fatigue of jobs for teenagers, young Americans usually attain a sense of invincibility with a job. Because of the consistent income from a job, young Americans may feel that school is not necessary anymore. They may sense that they can do anything they want because they are adults now and have incomes to survive. This sense of invincibility and complete independence is great for adults. However, it is extremely dangerous for young people.

With a sense of invincibility and independence, young Americans lose the obligations to go to school and succeed in education. They tend to feel that school is simply a stepping stone to a job. If they already have a job, they would not need to focus their times on a stepping stone any longer. Of course, this type of thinking does not occur all the time, especially among driven and ambitious students. They would probably work even harder at school because jobs for teenagers usually come with minimum wages. Unfortunately, not many young Americans are driven and ambitious enough to avoid such traps. I mean most teenagers in most countries aren't. That's the simple fact of life. I have to admit that most young Americans and young people in general do not have matured minds. They are falsely overjoyed with the jobs they already have in high school. Such mentality is quite frequent in today's society.

To me, the epitome to this outcome from a job is my friend Richard. Since my freshman year in high school, we have been great friends. At that time, I was the new kid at school who used to live in both China and

Canada. Since I did not know anyone, I was quite lonely.

Then a group of people approached me. They were my classmates from the Honors classes, and they offered to become my friends at school. Since then, we always sat together during lunch, and we always hanged out together. One of those people was Richard. He was one of the good students at school. We were in the same honors mathematics and biology classes together. When I first met Russell and got to know him, the most conspicuous quality about him was that he was very versatile. He was social, intelligent, musical, and athletic. In some ways, he was someone I looked up to as a role model. He was definitely one of the kids at school I could see as a successful individual in the future.

Our friendship grew stronger when we joined the same student organization at school, the Future Business Leaders of America. Since the organization required a lot of traveling, either to Indianapolis or Chicago, we spent a lot of time together.

It was our freshman year. We had a lot of fun traveling to all the places for conferences. During our times together, I learned a lot about Richard. He was very ambitious. He aspired to become a doctor in the future and attend an Ivy League school like MIT or Harvard. At the time, I did not doubt his abilities to do so. With his versatility and intelligence, he was definitely able to get accepted by an Ivy League school and become a doctor in the soon future. I envied both his well-rounded abilities and his great ambition. I respected his character, and he was quite a Renaissance man in my eyes.

When my sophomore year began, Richard and I remained friends. However, he decided to forgo the opportunity to rejoin the Future Business Leaders of

America organization that year. I was both shocked and sad about this news. He told me that he did not have time for extracurricular activities anymore because he just recently found a job at a fast food restaurant. I thought that the job would be great for him. He could really get in touch with the real world and prepare him for his future career as a doctor. But I was very wrong.

With his new job, he changed into a different kind of student. As months passed by, his original ambitions and dreams were gone. With the flight of his ambitions, his dedications to school and academic achievements disappeared as well. For a while, I was unable to find him at school and in the classrooms. Apparently, he missed a lot of school during his sophomore year.

For a while, I thought he was really ill. He was always one of the students who frequently catch illness, even in his freshman year. When he finally came back to school on several occasions, my other friends and I asked what happened to him. He told us that he had to work a lot. Since he already earned a lot of money at a restaurant, he told us that he felt it was unnecessary for him to focus on school anymore. He believed that he should focus on something with real substance like a job. All the hard works he paid would result in income. On the other hand, he felt that all the hard works he paid for school were kind of wasteful since all he got was a grade and nothing else like money. Additionally, Richard told us that he did not need school any longer. He already had a job, and it was enough for him to live independently and buy anything he wanted like video games. His feelings of invincibility and independence with his job in high school completely changed his point of view on education. Quite frankly, his job had additionally altered his path in his future and changed his perspective on life.

The same story has repeated consistently in the American education system. We have always seen changes to wonderful and ambitious young Americans in early years of high school. Later, as they qualify for jobs, many of those young people decided to drop education in exchange for short term income. No matter its fatigue or feeling of invincibility, this has been a serious problem existing in the American education system.

Of course, there are teenagers who actually find those jobs and think them as motivations. Not only do they not completely dedicating their lives to the part-time job, they can also realize that education can prevent them from receiving a similar job in the future. The desire for a better career and better salaries will definitely motivate farsighted and sage students. Who are we kidding? The jobs we get as teenagers are jokes! However, this does not happen in most cases. The young minds of American students including me sometimes are gullible and nearsighted. However, such inclination should be contained in the future in order to maintain competitive in a global economy.

Well, I know what you are asking yourself right now. What about the Chinese young people? Don't they face the same obstacles and realities? My answer to that is a definitive "no". In China, young people, especially those in high school, do not work. There are three main reasons to this reality.

First and foremost, majority of Chinese students are stuck in the same circumstance as I am. We are basically in the same boat. Although I live in America, my parents forbid me from acquiring any jobs outside during my high school years. They believe that having a job in high school will be a great distraction to my school work and my path to college. My parents who are wise and shrewd understand that having a job in high school will give me too much power and control on my decisions.

As a young person, I am prone to making foolish decisions such as placing work instead of school as my highest priority in life. Such decision has affected many young Americans, and my parents always try to prevent it from happening to me. This exact same train of thoughts also exists in the minds of many parents in China. Those parents all have high hopes for their children. Under the One Child Policy, the only child of the parents is like a piece of jewel. In order to keep those jewels valuable in the future, they need their children to further their education and to attain a higher education degree. Because of this type of thinking, they would almost never allow their children to work in high school—unless the family counts on the extra income for survival.

Another reason preventing young Chinese from getting jobs is the scarcity of job opportunities for them. In China, there are over 1.33 billion people. Even the adults in China with a college degree sometimes struggle with finding a job. Additionally, many quite strong and skilled adults are competing for blue-collar jobs at fast food restaurants and local restaurants. That's how competitive the job market can get. Even the educated sometimes move down and become fast food restaurant employees.

With the intensity and magnitude of the job competitions, the young people are simply not desirable to employers. To them, the young people lack experience, stability, focus, and physical strength. Even if the parents allow young Chinese to find jobs while in high school, there would be no employers in China who are willing to hire them and pay them. Additionally, the salaries in the United States are generally very high. Therefore many fast food restaurants hire young people in order to save money. In China, however, the wages are quite low, even for adults. Therefore, there are no reasons or incentives for employers to hire young people.

Last but not least, the disparity on the educational standards is another reason driving jobs away from young Chinese. In the United States, the schools are more liberal and laid-back with education. During school years, young Americans usually have a lot of free time because the schools don't usually bind students to complete dedication to education and homework.

Unlike United States, the Chinese educational standards are more rigorous. Students need to set aside a lot of time after school for homework and personal studies. Because of this rigorous education system, students like me in China do not have the opportunities to find jobs. If I were to attend a Chinese high school, I would be lucky if I were to complete all the assignments and be prepared for the next school day. A job would be a huge wildcard for Chinese students. On the contrary, as I mentioned earlier, having a job as a teenager in America is extremely common and realistic.

So how can American students stay away from the temptations jobs bring? There are several options. Of course, the best way to prevent distractions from jobs is to prohibit young Americans from ever getting a job in the first place. Despite its guaranteed effect, I would personally not recommend that. One great lesson I learned from the American education system is that there are more options outside of school. America truly provides an opportunity for young people to fully develop in all aspects of life—socially, academically, athletically, and experimentally.

Jobs for young people are great. They can be great tools to educate young people mentally, ethically, realistically, empirically, and socially. They provide an experimental edge for American young people on the international scene. To prevent overboard dedication, sense of invincibility, and altering priorities, the entire community—educators, parents, and students—should be aware of dangers to jobs. Through awareness, the entire community can bring a defensive approach to teenage jobs. When young people go overboard with their jobs, parents and educators, through awareness of the danger, can quickly detect and correct. Sometimes, the greatest wrong doings in life are inattention and inaction.

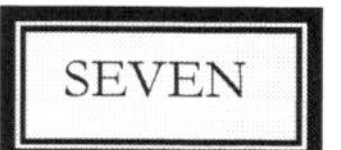

All for One, One for All

When people discuss the unwitting determinations and dedications of Chinese young people on education and career success, people tend to find the obvious. They only see such phenomenon as the result of the Chinese parents' never-ending naggings and scolding. As a Chinese teenager, I have to say that's quite true! My parents do nag about my laid-back attitudes toward education and life. But there's more depth to that.

When we discuss dedication and determination, I found that many Americans see it on a personal level. While their dedications and competitive natures are very personal and idiosyncratic, there is another unforeseen side to this phenomenon. This unforeseen side is the Chinese national pride.

Chinese national pride is a more euphemistic version of Chinese nationalism. And this national pride is very different from the American patriotism many of you are familiar with. Many of you may think that this is weird and exotic, but it is true that many Chinese people today including young ones pursue success in order to preserve the national pride and honor of their nation.

In America, I learned that many Americans are very patriotic. They like to wear flag pins and to pay respects to soldiers who fight battles oversea. Americans love to talk about how wonderful United States is, and many young Americans have to recite the pledge of allegiance to the flag every day. As a student, I know this very well! Of course, Americans from every corner of the nation celebrate July Fourth or Independence Day with joy and pride. However, the Chinese national pride and nationalism is on a whole other level compared to American patriotism.

There are many ways to explain the disparity on the degree of national pride. For one, Chinese young people have a whole week off in October during China's Independence Celebration. In contrast, Americans only have one day off on July 4th.

On a more serious note, the foundation and social fabric disparity between the two world powers have deeply impacted the degree of national pride. America is a melting-pot. It was originally found by the Europeans who persecuted the Native Americans, or the American Indians. Later, people from different areas of the world have made up this nation and called themselves "Americans." Although this group of "Americans" loves this country very much and enjoys its opportunities, their nationalistic feelings and national prides are not as strong and passionate as those of the Chinese. Sometimes, the immigrants coming into America remain loyal to their native countries. This has caused an overall decrease in national pride, loyalty, and nationalistic sentiment.

China is a more traditional country with a very conventional social makeup. Although there are many minority groups in China (technically 56 different groups), they are all considered oriental and were all descended from the same region called China. Throughout the rich Chinese history, this group of people, despite coming from different minority groups, stood as one and faced foreign invaders with courage. Many times, they all have suffered through persecution and humiliation caused by groups like the Europeans, the Japanese, and the Americans. From their shared suffering and humiliation, Chinese people have formed a very special and unbreakable bond. They saw themselves as the victims of imperialism. They shared anguishes. Those unfortunate and shameful pasts allowed them to realize that only a united and formidable China can prevent them from further sufferings and humiliations in the future.

Because of the shared anguish and cultural background, Chinese people, especially young people, are taught to make China proud. They have senses of vengeance from their hurtful history. They want to seek satisfaction and redemption through the success of China on the world stage. They want to see China as a powerful nation because it will be a direct reflection on the Chinese race and Chinese culture.

Chinese young people today carry two burdens unlike many American young people. They have to be successful for personal pride and personal livelihood. They also have to succeed in education and career to add another bright spot on China's world image. In America, young people do not sense the burden of the nation because the country has been at the top of the world for decades. Young Americans have already taken the nation's success and strength for granted and have never experienced national anguish like Chinese young people do.

The makeup of the population is a critical effect to the degree of national pride. As I mentioned earlier, since America is an immigration destination, almost all Americans have been from another country—no matter if they are first or second or third generation. In some degrees, Americans do not have as much loyalty to the country as Chinese do. Parts of Americans' loyalty belong to their home countries where either they were from or their ancestors were from.

Obviously, I am not saying that Americans do not love their country. Of course, they do. However, the extent of loyalty compared to that of Chinese is comparatively less. From my experience, Chinese people live and accomplish for themselves and for their home country, China. This sense of national mission is always imbedded in the minds of Chinese people through their years of education. Even if the Chinese has already moved out of the country for years, the unbreakable bond still exists between the person and China. I cannot even explain this phenomenon with a logical reason. There are too many factors that contribute to this great and united bond among Chinese.

In my family, this sense of loyalty to China remains very strong. I sometimes think that there is this invisible string that unwittingly connects my family with our ancestral nation. As I have mentioned in the previous chapters, my family immigrated to North America in 2002. We have been Canadian citizens since 2006 and residents of United States for three years. During this period of time, we have developed a keen sense of love and loyalty for both Canada and United States. We are very appreciative of the opportunities both countries have provided us.

Both Canada and United States offered my father ample opportunities to succeed and to excel in his career field. My mother benefited by gaining an opportunity to attend a North American higher education institution and to reestablish her career path. I benefited the most. By moving here, I have the option to learn from a more balanced and more laid-back education system in America. Most importantly, I finally gained the courage to dream again in the "land of the brave." Despite our gratefulness and love of both Canada and United States, the invisible knot between my family and China never loosened.

During the 2008 Beijing Olympics, our Chinese loyalty and national pride were put to test. This is quite silly for many of you, but the Summer Olympics is very important in my family. It's like the biggest sports event!

As many Olympics spectators may know, China and United States are the two dominant forces in the Summer Olympics. The previous Olympics in Athens placed China as second on the gold medal ranking and United States as first. Without doubts, the rivalry continued during the Beijing Olympics. Prior to the game, I thought that both my parents and I would most definitely root for the American athletes since we have been living here for so long. Unknowingly, we were completely wrong with our initial assumption.

I have to confess that I rooted for China and detested United States during the Beijing Olympics Game. I tried my hardest to root for both sides; however, my natural instincts and feelings got the best of me. The detestations I had for United States Olympics team are not the result of my dissatisfaction with the country. I love the country. But I wanted China to be first on the gold medal ranking, and the US was the only challenger for that position.

Those feelings I had were beyond my control. During the Women's Gymnastic Group final, China and United States were the teams contending for the gold medal. I can vividly remember this because this was one of the biggest events showcasing Chinese-American Olympics rivalry. Although I loved Shawn Johnson, Nastia Liukin, and the entire women's gymnastics team, my Chinese national pride had the better of me. I was overjoyed when the Chinese women's gymnastics team won. Later, when American news networks claimed that the Chinese female gymnasts were underage, my Chinese national pride made me furious and paranoid. I can still recall how funny it was when my mother got all red and complained about the American media's biases on the controversial topic. It was fun to observe, but it also said everything about this bond we have to China.

Even though my feelings during Beijing Olympics can be quite humorous and insignificant, they clearly delineate and demonstrate the ties Chinese people today have for their home country. Even for people like my family who have been living in a foreign nation for years, we still have a strong sense of Chinese nationalism and national pride.

Sometimes, my accomplishments in America make me proud. From those accomplishments, I knew that I made China look good in front of the world. Sometimes, I feel burdened to succeed in America because I knew that I have the burden of an entire nation upon my shoulder. This type of feeling and responsibility is not unique for me. Almost all Chinese people both in China and out of China have the exact same mentality and exact same sense of burden and responsibility.

You may ask how do national pride and nationalism lead to young Chinese's dedication to education and career success. For me, this answer is very easy and very clear. Because young Chinese today have a strong sense of national pride, they have profound and heavy responsibilities. They know that in order to make China successful on the world stage, each of them has to contribute. Each of them has to succeed in a particular field. They know that if all Chinese people do the same, China can be more united and can have a group of outstanding talents who can progress the nation in the future. This mentality drives and burdens young people in China to work harder and to study harder for success. Unfortunately, those burdens and responsibilities do not exist in America due to historical and cultural disparity.

One possible reason for America's lessened version of national pride and nationalism may be the foundation of government. In China, there are many parties. This may be surprising, but this fact is true. However, as we all know, there is one dominant party, which is the Communist Party. No matter what one may feel about the Chinese government, it's undeniable that it has done a great job unifying the country. There are few dissents because of their lack of options and limited freedom of speech.

No matter what one perceives on the morality of this type of government, it's definite that it has worked in China. To some extent, Chinese government has controlled the media very well and has successfully promoted a sense of national pride through personal success and responsibility. This type of promotion cannot happen in America, and that's partly the reason that young Americans do not have the burden to work hard for the country.

In America, as we all know, there are two main political parties. The government has been very democratic and very genuine with freedom of speech. Since there are two oppositional parties in the country, there will always be a group of dissents who are dissatisfied with the country and the government (usually the party loyalties of a failed presidential campaign). Because there are constant disagreements between the factions, the country as a whole has created a dynamic of division. This dynamic has deeply influenced American young people and decreased their sense of national pride. Sometimes, they may feel discontentment toward the government and loses their senses of responsibility and national pride. This loss of responsibility and national pride compromises young Americans' will to succeed in education and career for the good of the country. This pattern has occurred throughout American history, and this may have also contributed to the lack of motivation American young people have for education and career success.

In contrast, the Chinese nationalism and national pride have seen a new wave of resurgence in modern times. In the 1990s, the end of the Cold War brought in a new type of Chinese nationalism, the positive nationalism. During this period of time, the emerged intellectual class popularized the notion that China can be successful without having hard power and the supports of the radical communist faction. The educated group of people realized that China as a nation could finally emerge as a superpower if its people unite and use their ingenuities to shape the country. Since then, the idea has been publicized throughout China. Today, this idea of national pride through personal success has become second-nature to the Chinese, especially the young Chinese.

Today, the Chinese nationalism has reached its zenith. During the Beijing Olympics, controversies with Tibet have aroused strong nationalistic sentiments from both native and oversea Chinese. This phenomenon is true no matter what position one supports. One can always find people holding signs saying "One China" during all major events around the world such as the Olympics Torch Relay. This demonstration illustrates the strong sense of national pride the Chinese race possesses at the moment.

Since then, national pride continued to increase. The devastating earthquake that took place in Sichuan further aroused unity and nationalistic sentiments throughout China. Both the Olympics Game and the earthquake are testaments on how Chinese people today take pride in the success of China and want to continue to expand this success through personal endeavors.

The relationship between national pride and Chinese young people's will for success in both education and careers may seem far reaching for many Americans today. Yet this relationship is very true. Not only have I felt the same way throughout my life, there are countless Chinese teenagers today with similar feelings. No matter it's a demonstration during a Chinese controversy or a natural disaster, Chinese people today have demonstrated their love and passion for their home nation. This tie is still very strong and unbreakable.

Unlike China, the inherent American philosophies have prevented Americans from having strong national pride. Even when we examine the United States Constitution, we can see that the country was founded with a focus on the individuals. Everything in the Constitution was based on an intention to protect the individual rights instead of national prosperity. American philosophy is individualistic while the Chinese philosophy is nationalistic. The disparity in philosophy directly contributes to today's difference.

For Americans, attaining such a level of national pride is very difficult due to the foundation of the nation and its environment in general. However, it's not impossible. As I lived in this great nation with many great promises and opportunities, I quickly learned the dynamic. It's very different from China. In China, people think both as individuals and as a part of a unit called

China. In America, people only think and make decisions as individuals. The American dynamic is very chaotic because every individual has a very different agenda in life. Sometimes, one individual's agenda conflicts with another's. It's almost impossible to move a nation forward, including young people, if chaos and different goals sit in the same environment.

In order to combat this reality, this is the time for all Americans to get united and think for the better of the nation. This is especially true for young people. In America, young people only think about competing against their peers in America. They forget about uniting and working as a team facing international competition. This mentality and demeanor have to change before great progress. When young Americans think in a united way and work with other young Americans, they will also develop a great sense of national pride. With that sense of national pride, they are looking to do great things in life.

Faith and the Faithless

"What do I believe? As an American I believe in generosity, in liberty, in the rights of man. These are social and political faiths that are part of me, as they are, I suppose, part of all of us. Such beliefs are easy to express. But part of me too is my relation to all life, my religion." A famous American politician, Adlai E. Stevenson, uttered those words of wisdom in a speech given on May 21, 1954 in Libertyville, Illinois.

Adlai Stevenson was a very clever man. His point of view on Americans and their faiths demonstrated one of the essences on the difference between Chinese and American young people today. It's very simple. American young people grew in an environment with faith—both social and religious faith. Chinese young people, on the other hand, have not.

Don't get me wrong. I am not claiming that Chinese young people don't have any faith or religious beliefs at all. They do! I was one of them few years ago, and I have to admit that I had strong faith back then—maybe just a different kind of faith. From my observations, the faith and religious beliefs of Chinese young people are conspicuously different from those of American young people.

In America, young Americans have a balance on purpose in life. They live both for the present and for the future—future as an afterlife. From my experience in America, I found that the Christian faith of many young Americans has inspired them to live a more well-rounded life. From the general Christian teaching, many young Americans hold a strong belief that there is a heaven after death. Such belief has been stamped into the minds of young Americans either through their family or the Christian atmosphere in America. Because of this very belief, young Americans are constrained in some ways to please God through good works and dedication to the Christian values. As young Americans progress through life from youth to adulthood, their Christian values and beliefs hinder them from dedicating their entire time to education and the drive for career success.

I have been living in North America for over six years and in United States for three of those years. While I was living here, I became a Christian and adapted to the American daily routine. On Sundays, my family usually goes to church like many American young people's families. On week days, we often enjoy our times studying the Bible and many other Christian teachings.

As a result of those activities, Christian education has been added to my usually hectic schedule that includes my traditional studies at school. On many occasions, I remember giving up time from school work and personal academic training for my Christian faith. Additionally, there are usually church gatherings, which I have to dedicate more of my time to. Because of the frenzied schedule dedicated to my Christian faith, my dedication to education has dramatically decreased compared to my dedication back in China. While other Chinese young people today are challenging themselves harder and harder on academic achievements, I have to create a balance in my life and decrease my dedication for school education. This is a fact of life. You gain some, and you lose some.

Even if going to church on a Sunday is not part of a young American's schedule, the Christian atmosphere is contagious. Because most American young people believe in heaven, they want to do activities in order to be one of the chosen ones. Those activities include family time, service to the church, volunteering, and time with friends. The activities mentioned are strongly advocated by the Christian teaching, and they can take a lot of time out of a person's life.

From Christian faith and those activities involved, young Americans have to prioritize and balance unlike their Chinese counterparts. The diversity of their activities due to their Christian faith has taken away time for studying and dedication in a specific field such as Chemistry and Physics. This shift in priority due to faith has caused young Chinese to move ahead academically.

Unlike the Americans, Chinese young people live more monotonously. Because of the inherit conditions, China is not very open to religion. That's why Chinese young people are not very religious and mostly are ignorant of the concept of heaven.

I can still remember my days in China. While I was living there, I was never introduced to religion. I never in a million years would have thought that there was a possibility of a God out there. Since religion was never part of my life or part of my family's life, I never had any religious faith. Sometimes, I thought about death, but the way of thinking was completely different than most American young people. I was convinced that after a person died, he or she would be buried in the ground in a state of unconsciousness. I always thought that death would be the end of the line for a person's journey in life. I was ignorant of the possibility of heaven and God. Although my perceptions and lack of experience with religion came at quite a young age, I am absolutely sure that similar ideas have invaded the minds of many Chinese young people like me today.

The lack of faith completely transformed Chinese young people's lifestyle and priorities in life. It has further distinguished Chinese students from American students. Due to a lack of exposal to religion, Chinese people in general live for the present instead of the future in the form of afterlife. They believe that their time on earth will be the only time they will exist. Therefore, it's their duty to make the most out of their time on earth and to succeed in any way possible. I have to confess that I was one of them who had a very similar train of thought.

Since I did not have any religious faith when I lived in China, I never thought about pleasing someone like God while living my life. This idea affected me and my lifestyle in a variety of ways. I misleadingly believed that I never needed to dedicate my time to church or religion since there was none. Those times were used for studying and my pursuit of success in life.

While many young people in America went to church on Sundays, I as a Chinese youth stayed home and dedicated all those time to math, science, Chinese, and philosophy. I thought that the present life was all I needed to live for, and success in this life was very crucial for me. Of course, I am not going to settle whether there is a God out there. No one knows for sure. However, believing can have a great impact on a person's life. On the contrary, not believing has a similar effect as well. My earlier lack of understanding for religion and Christian faith was a reflection of such impact.

In addition to increased time for education, my atheist views at that time made me somewhat "ruthless" compared to American young people. I believed that the only power that could control me was my own abilities and my own weaknesses. I thought that I was the only one that could control my success in life. Because of such responsibility and lack of religious faith, I placed higher education and monetary success as the only way to happiness in life (of course, Christian values in America have taught all of us that education and monetary success are not the only ways to achieve happiness). My ignorance of this idea made me "ruthless" and allowed me to strive a lot harder in education compared to the more religious and influenced minds of Americans. I was going to do everything I could to achieve monetary success.

Although I cannot speak for all Chinese, my thoughts and my experiences at the time must be very similar to many Chinese young people today. As we all know, one's religious faith can shape one's life. In similar ways, one's lack of religious faith can alter one's life as well. Because Chinese young people are not introduced to religious faiths and values like Christianity, they are not as consumed in time and priorities as their American counterparts. Therefore, they have more time and dedication for education and personal endeavors.

I know what many of you are thinking right now. What about Buddhism? Isn't that very popular in China? Yes, it is! But its effects in China are very different than Christianity's effects in America.

In China, Buddhism is more of a superstition than a religion. Although there are still many true Buddhists in China, the majority of Chinese who go to temples and pray to Buddha aren't. I can still remember the times when my family and I were one of those people. We did believe in the power of Buddha, but it was more superstitious.

Every holiday season, my family and I went to a local temple and made donations to Buddha. In return, many of us prayed or, in many cases, implored for good fortune. My parents asked for better jobs and better pays. My grandparents asked for a closer family. My uncle begged for more money so he could finally move out of his parents' apartment. I asked for better grades at school. In simple terms, we as "Buddhists" were selfish believers. Instead of gaining a religious faith and conducting good works with those faiths, we were simply sitting around and occasionally pray for what we wanted. Our "religious faith" in China never really consumed our times, and we never had to give up much in exchange for our "religious faith."

Although this is not the same for every family, I can almost guarantee you that majority of people in China who claim to be Buddhists are not really Buddhists. They all have selfish needs like my family at that time, and Buddhism was a superstition to attain those wants and needs.

More importantly, the Buddhist culture of China inspired people to work even harder for money and for better education. In America, Christianity requires people, especially young people, to take time and to conduct good works. Those works sidetrack Americans from completely focusing on education and monetary success. In China, Buddhism only requires several donations and visits to a temple per year in order to advance people's selfish interests. Instead of teaching better values and diversifying one's goals in life, Buddhism has been enhancing the desires for higher education and monetary success in China. Today's Chinese culture and the competitive nature of Chinese young people are partially the products of this unconventional "Buddhist" culture.

As a disclaimer, I want to be quite clear. The "Buddhist" culture and practice in China, on most occasions, are not the real faith and demeanors of Buddhists. I do not want to offend any real Buddhists out there with real faiths and dedications to the religion.

When I was brainstorming on the effects of religious faith on young people and their focus on education, one name immediately jumped into my mind. This name is David.

David is a good friend of mine. As a matter of fact, we still attend the same high school together. He was one of the first people I met after my move to the United States. My initial impression of David was his wonderful and delightful demeanors. Since I attend a public high school, his actions made him stand out among his peers. Even today, he is respectful and polite. He helps out around the Special Education department at my school. His best friend is actually a lovely girl who lost her sight due to an unfortunate genetic disease. After a few days at the new school, I quickly predicted that David was a young man with great religious faith and values. And I was correct.

He is definitely a great friend and a wonderful Christian. Through the three years of knowing him, I got to know him quite well. By no means is he an exemplary Christian at my school. There are more devout and more dedicated ones in my high school. In many ways, he is simply a typical Midwestern American student with a strong religious faith. He attends churches on a consistent basis. From what I know, he always attends church service on Sundays and often attends weekday services as well. He is also an active member of the church. He always participates in church volunteer activities, and he always volunteers on behalf of his church as well. Since we are friends, he always invites me to join his church youth group. Sometimes I feel bad that I have to reject his invitations because of prior engagements. However, I fully see his dedications to his church and his religious faith.

So why am I telling a story about David? Well, his religious faith and activities with the church often affected his focus and dedications on school work and academic achievements. We have been going to the same classes for the past three years. I know exactly how intelligent David is. He is one of the smartest people I have ever met. Of course, when I say "smart", I mean naturally and innately intelligent. He is one of those students who do not have to take notes and try extremely hard at school and still comprehend the materials.

Last year, we were in the same AP Chemistry class together. The general consensus is that AP Chemistry is the hardest course at my high school. But it was definitely not for David. He sailed through the course as if it was an elementary course. In class, everyone was taking notes and listening to the instructor attentively. I can always hear frustrations and sounds of giving up during the class. Although I rank top in my class academically, I was frustrated on most occasions during the class period. Many students did not know, but I usually studied like a crazy person before each Chemistry test. As a result, I often received one of the highest grades in the class. But it truly came from hard works and absolute dedication. On the other hand, David often received a top score on assessments as well, and he never studied. All he did was listening to all the intricate Chemistry concepts in class and comprehending them all. That's how smart this guy is. Sometimes, I envy his intelligence.

Despite David's fantastic mind, he is not the valedictorian of my class. As a matter of fact, he does not even rank in the top 10. Sometimes I am surprised that I rank number 1 when naturally smarter American students like David are in the same class. The only reason that David does not rank in the top 10 academically is his preoccupation with his religious faith. I have experienced several occasions when he failed to finish his homework because of his hectic schedule with his church. Of course, homework and assignments always make up a huge portion of one's grade at school. Missing assignments have dramatically lowered David's academic achievements at school. He is not achieving his full potential because of his religious faith. He simply cannot place all his time and focus on school. Sometimes, I pity this reality. However, I also respect his religious devotions.

Discussing the effects of religion on American students puts me in a rock and a hard place. On one hand, I cannot deny religion's role in diminishing young Americans' focuses on education and career success. On the other hand, I cannot really criticize and scold religion for having such an effect. For many of us, religion is simply too important and too valuable. For many, it's greater than life and greater than education and career success. This type of condition usually leads to very controversial debates. Yet we must not back down and ignore its effects. I do not want to suggest young Americans to give up their religious faith as a tradeoff for academic success. Nevertheless an awareness of its role in education and lives of American young people is critical. Such awareness can not only answer many questions, but also provides an opportunity for American families to correctly face challenges and distractions in their own ways.

In addition to religious faith, there is another genre of faith that contributes to the Chinese-American disparity. When we talk about faith, people usually think about religious faith—faith with God. However, we often leave out a very important type of faith—social faith.

Such faith was mentioned in the quote of Adlai Stevenson at the beginning of the chapter. He truly understands Americans. He knows that what makes Americans unique is their social faith of freedom and equality. It was until I moved here to America when I realized the real meaning of freedom, equality, and opportunity for the pursuit of happiness. I never experienced social faith like this in China. Just like young Americans' familiarities with such social faith, I can bet that Chinese young people today are strangers to those ideas and faiths.

When I was an elementary school student in China, I only knew one way to succeed. There was only one narrow path for every one of us in China. This path was an educational path. Back in the days, the only activity a young person needs to do is to study. It was our social obligation. Such obligation was promoted in the entire Chinese culture. I learned it through constant reminders of my family, especially my parents, and the Chinese pop culture. Even cartoons usually subliminally remind young Chinese to study hard in order to succeed.

The entire Chinese culture was fabricated upon a narrow point view and a myopic social faith. Because the Chinese society never promoted other options other than education, education has been the Holy Grail for a successful life in China. In many cases, education is the only option for a decent livelihood—not to mention great success. Because the entire culture is based upon this one path and one goal, no one dares to get sidetracked. Unfortunately many do not make it through the educational path successfully. But it is not because of lack of efforts. Sometimes the overwhelming competitions and personal inabilities facing such competitions result in the failures along the way.

Today Chinese young people are taking this similar intensity to the international stage. That's why American young people today are being pressured to work harder in order to compete with them. That's also why many Americans today are anxious about the future when their posterities have to face the robotic-like competitions from countries like China and India. Yet many do not realize that the competitive nature of the Chinese is not new. They have always existed, even when I was in China in the 1990s.

In the past, the intensity of Chinese young people was within the border of China. Due to swift globalization and emergence of China as a world power, those young people with a monotonous social faith in education see opportunities on the international level. Since they have already gained the edge in valuing education and seeing it as the only option to success, their talents in academic areas such as math and science have currently overwhelmed and surprised Americans of similar age.

However, the surprise of Americans on Chinese young people's academic excellence does not surprise me at all. This is especially true after living in the country for many years. In America, I found that American young people have diversity in social faiths. They can believe in freedom, equality, and countless opportunities to succeed. I cannot say the same for Chinese young people.

Because the country was found with diversity in social faiths, American young people have many options in front of them to succeed in life. They can pursue happiness and success in so many different ways that Chinese young people can never dream of. As an American resident, I personally benefited from the diversity of options inspired by the ideals of American social faith.

When I first moved to America, I was a very shy and uncertain boy. In China, dedication to education was the only goal in my life. Since education was the only path to success in my home country, I was very skeptical about my future. At school, I was a good student, but never an exceptional student. Even at a small elementary school, I could not claim that I was the best student in the school. Knowing that education was the only way for me to succeed, I developed a very average dream. I simply wanted to become a technical employee like many of my family members.

The reason for my below-average dream was the lack of social faith that exists in China. Education was the only way to judge a person's success, and I was not one of the best at it. I felt trapped and limited by the lonely path for success called education. Although I was inherently very loquacious, creative, and witty as a child, I never had the opportunity to utilize them. As a matter of fact, I never knew many of my talents until I moved to America.

The uncertainty arrived with me when I first landed in North America. Originally, I thought that the American culture was very similar to the Chinese culture. Therefore, my perceptions about my future never changed on the day I arrived. In the past six to seven years in America, my original social faith changed and developed dramatically. I realized that America is a nation where any person can succeed no matter what talents he or she has. In this country, anything is possible because there are freedom, equality, and countless opportunities. Young Americans are not limited to the path of education.

Today, I still value education as an important aspect of my life. However, my American social faith made me value other options as well. I learned that I have other paths to success in America. My entire experience in this country has opened up my eyes and allowed me to see the world beyond education and academic achievements. If America never provided me with diverse social faith and paths to success, I would never been able to write this book at this very moment!

Without any doubts, Chinese young people today are far ahead of American young people in education and academic reaching. This should not be surprising because they don't have the richness in faith like American young people have. Their lack of faith allows them to dedicate countless hours to education. That's why there are so many intelligent scientists and engineers produced in China today. They are competing with Americans and trying to take jobs away from them. If Americans have to blame this disadvantaged situation, they should blame their strong faiths and values! That's some irony! Isn't it?

When I was observing the differences on faith between Americans and Chinese, I saw a very interesting pattern. Chinese young people are actually gaining an advantage and a rare competitive edge through lack of faith and complete dedication to education. American young people, however, are actually facing a disadvantage in those areas with the addition of social faiths. As an observer, this pattern is very disturbing and frustrating.

I personally believe that faith in a young person's life is excellent and can be very beneficial to his or her education. What we have observed today is an incorrect use of faith. In America today, many young people are using faith as an escape. For religious faith, they use it as an excuse to avoid school works. Many times, young Americans simply replace education with faith. They do not balance and tend to go for the extreme. For social faith, they take advantage of the options and opportunities, and use them to their disadvantage. I think this misuse of opportunities and faiths are simply devastating. To me, this is like having a pot of gold and throwing it into the ocean.

One Child Policy

The year 1979 was a very eventful year in the United States. In March, the US President Jimmy Carter successfully convinced long time foes, Egypt and Israel, to sign a peace treaty called the Camp David Accord. That same month, Pennsylvania experienced one of the most traumatic nuclear power plant accidents in history at a place called Three Mile Island. Later in 1979, the Iranian Hostage Crisis broke the hearts of every American. Everyone was worried about the Americans trapped at the Iranian-American embassy. Internationally, the US finally opened up a complete diplomatic relation with China. Although it was a monumental year in American history, the Chinese had more plans for 1979 than a new diplomatic relation with United States. The Chinese, that year, introduced a new policy called the One Child Policy that would have dramatic effects in the years to come.

What is the One Child Policy? The answer is quite self-explanatory. It was a law created by the Chinese government to limit most couples in China to one offspring. Although there are still some exceptions in the rural regions of China, this policy has dramatically cut down on population growth and limited many Chinese families today to one child. In the years following its implementation, many councils and agencies were formed to deal with the enforcement. Many communities in China used family planning programs to insure couples to stay under the quota. Additionally, abortions increased in order to obey the law.

So why did China implement such a program? In many ways, it was absolutely necessary before worse disasters occur. In 1979, China faced a major dilemma. Its population was growing at an overwhelming rate. The country's capabilities at the time were unable to keep up with the growth of the population. According to many scientific analysts at the time, China could face major tragedies and problems if the country did not act to prevent further population expansion. With the One Child Policy, the Chinese government intended to alleviate social, economic, and environmental problems that would be inevitable without slowing down population growth.

Now we have grasped the basics of the One Child Policy. But still, what does a law in China contributes to the difference between Chinese and American students on educational excellence? Honestly, the contribution is great.

I want to first tell a story that happened when I was nine years old. I was living with my grandparents, my uncle, and my uncle's wife in a small apartment in the city of Anshan. My uncle and his wife were married for two years, and they struggled financially. They were forced to live with my grandparents. Because of the same financial difficulties, they did not attempt to have a child immediately after marriage. Under such circumstance, I was the only child in the family.

Every day, my grandparents, my uncle, and his wife were revolving part of their time on me. My grandparents strictly implemented my study plan on a daily basis. The study plan was created with the involvements of my parents who were then living in another city working in big firms. Since I was the only child in the family, everyone dedicated their focus on me. While my grandparents were strictly enforcing the study plans, my uncle sometimes tutored me with some basic mathematics problems. Almost everyone living with me was active with my education. Everyone disciplined me and set strict rules for my actions. Even my allowances for school were limited to certain amounts. It was like 1 to 2 Yuan per day.

When I turned 10 years old, a dramatic event happened. My uncle and his wife had a baby. Although he was just my cousin, we lived under the same roof, and it seemed like that I had a brother in the family. The arrival of a new child in the family changed the whole dynamic. I was no longer the one who everyone paid attentions to. As a matter of fact, the baby required so much work that my grandparents, my uncle, and my aunt often neglected my education. Instead of focusing solely on me, they spread their focuses onto my new cousin.

The shift in focus allowed me to relax on my school works. My guardians at the time no longer strictly enforced the study plans. Of course, I was excited as a kid. I was no longer smothered by my guardians and their restraints on what I can do and cannot do. Additionally, I got more allowances. Instead of just 1 to 2 Yuan, I vividly remember that my grandmother gave me 5 Yuan on a daily basis. In some ways, I felt that money was a way for me to keep busy while they had to deal with the new baby.

Because of the new child in the family, my grades at school began to drop. Instead of scoring high 90s and 100s on my finals, I began to make low 90s and high 80s on those finals. The main reason for the decline in my educational excellence was the new child. The new child took away all the attentions I used to receive as an only child in the family. Because there were lesser attentions on me, I could slack off on my study plans and have more freedoms with my grades at school. Even when I had a bad grade at school, I was sometimes able to get away with it because the family had too much work to do. In addition to their own careers, they also had to deal with two children. Therefore, the overwhelming workloads then led to less enforcement on the rules and less focus on my educational achievements.

This same dynamic has differentiated the Chinese students from the American students. In the United States, most families have more than one child. As a matter of fact, I personally know many American families with 5 or 6 children. This type of family structure is a major reason why American students are not as competitive academically as many Chinese students living in China. Unlike China with its One Child Policy, United States does not have any limits on the number of children per family. Sometimes, there are even families with over 14 children. I can recall watching an American mother on television who recently had 8 babies at once. If she were in China, she would be in a lot of trouble! She would not even afford the fines for going over the quota!

As we have seen from my experience in a two children family, having more than one child per family can dramatically affect the educational achievements of children at school. In America, the students mostly live in families with more than one child. In addition to work, the parents have to deal with all the children. They are simply overwhelmed. Naturally, more than one child forces the parents to focus on multiple children at the same time.

The quality of such parenting can never be as good as the quality of parenting only one child. With one child, the parents can really focus on everything the child goes through and closely follow his or her footsteps at schools. With multiple children, the parents have to divert their attentions to different children. Diversion always leads to the parents leaving some children behind while focusing on one of the children.

In a family with two or more children, the children will always have times when they are free of strict discipline because the parents have to multitask all the time. During those times, the children may follow their primal instincts and do what they want to do. With such freedom, their educational achievements at school would obviously decline. Most students would probably take advantage of those times and use leisure as a replacement for more academic studying.

Unlike the United States, China has a different dynamic. With the One Child Policy, most Chinese families only have one child in the family. They live in a situation similar to my situation prior to the birth of my cousin. The parents can always dedicate all their times and focuses on one child. With this undivided attention, the child is usually very well disciplined. He or she will always be scolded if he or she fails on a school assignment or test. He or she will always be pushed into a strict set of study schedule. If he or she were to get sidetracked, the parents with their undivided attentions will always see it and make correct adjustments. This dynamic in China has raised a group of academically inclined and accomplished young people. As a result, they become very well trained in different career areas. They are ready to challenge their American counterparts because they know that they have been better prepared due to the disciplines of their parents and the school system.

While diversion of attention is a downside of bigger families, there is another reason why having more than one child may lead to decline in educational achievements among students. This reason is the lack of intensity in educating children within a bigger family.

In China, students are better prepared for education and their career fields because the parents have invested a lot in them. The Chinese One Child Policy not only limited the number of children Chinese couples can have, but it also limits the opportunities for Chinese parents to fulfill their obligations and life goals as individuals.

For parents, this is very true. After talking to my parents, I realized that as people grow older, they don't live just for fun. They also live to fulfill many life's goals. For many parents, one such goal is to successfully raise their children. In the end, through their education, dedications, and love, the parents hope to raise a child who is intelligent, successful, respectful, educated, and healthy. This is the dream of every parent both in America and in China. As a matter of fact, this dream is sort of universal for all parents in the world.

Unfortunately for the Chinese parents, this dream can only be fulfilled with one chance and one opportunity. The government only allows one child per couple through the One Child Policy. To them, this one chance is too important and too valuable. In order to guarantee that this one child will be successful, the parents would go out of their ways and place their undivided attentions on the child throughout his or her development. This includes the education of the child.

In China, older generations like the parents hold a belief that education is the best and probably the only way for success. To guarantee the fulfillment of their life's goal, they need to make sure that the child will succeed in school. Every day, Chinese parents would hover over their child and pressure him or her to focus on school. They do not allow their child to slack off at any moment of his or her school career. If he or she does sidetrack from education, the Chinese parents who constantly look over their child will find out and immediately correct the child from distracting behaviors.

To the parents, the One Child Policy has limited their chances to fulfill their obligations as parents and to achieve their life's goal. This pressure is usually transferred from the parents to the child. The parents want to have the best result with the only opportunity they have. This is similar to taking a standardized test. If there is only one shot at succeeding on the test, the test taker would take a lot of time studying. On test day, the test taker would also be very careful with answering the questions. He or she knows that there is no other chance for redemption. The test will determine everything, and he or she has to live with the result the rest of his or her life. That's pressure, and most people would take it very seriously.

On the other hand, if there are multiple opportunities to take a test like the SAT and ACT in the United States, the test taker would most likely take it easy, especially on the first few tests. Knowing that there will be more opportunities for redemption even if he or she fails on the test, the pressure is off. Sometimes, this mentality and this circumstance result in bad test scores on the first few tests. In this metaphor, American parents represent the latter situation.

In the United States, there are no restrictions on the number of children per family. There is no One Child Policy in America. For somewhat reason, the country actually encourages bigger families. Because of this circumstance, many American parents have more than one child. Most often, they have 3 or 4 children. With 2 or more children, American parents do not have to share the same pressures the Chinese parents have to face.

Although both groups of parents share the same dreams of having their children succeeding as adults and as students, they have uneven odds in achieving this dream. As I have discussed earlier, the Chinese parents only have one chance. This one chance is a great burden. This burden and pressure are then transferred to the child through the undivided attentions and disciplines of the parents.

Unlike the Chinese, American parents are fortunate to have multiple opportunities. If one child were to fail at school or fail in his or her career, this is not the end. The American parents would most often have another shot with another child. To them, the failure of one child does not represent the end. If they raise another child who succeeds at school and with his or her career, not only will the parents fulfill their goals in life and lift their burdens and obligations as parents, they will also have sibling supports for the previous children who did not succeed.

Because of such circumstance with so many chances, American parents are not as hardcore and strict as the Chinese parents on their children's education and future plans. They provide more options, more choices, and more freedoms to their children. On the other side of the globe, the Chinese parents try to limit those privileges in order to increase the chance of success with their one child.

It's hard to believe that a simple law can alter the path of two groups of people. Yet it's very true and very real today. The One Child Policy has further ramifications than simply decreasing the population of China. It has created a group of very cautious and much focused parents who would raise their one child with intensity and with strict discipline. In return, those children become very well trained for global competition with their outstanding skills in their respective career fields.

Because United States does not have such a law, the parents become more laid-back and less strict on their children. In the end, who would ever imagine that the controversial and somewhat immoral One Child Policy has strengthened the qualities of young Chinese? Likewise, who would ever believe that freedom and options without limitations from One Child Policy in America created a group of young people who are less prepared to face competition from China and other countries like India? That's some ironic reality I cannot even fathom, and I thought I was a smart guy!

Single vs. Diverging Priority

The difference between American and Chinese teenagers is significant. One important factor on such disparity is a difference on priority. As we all know, how a person lives his or her life depends solely on how he or she prioritizes. One's priority allows one to be more focused on one aspect of life and to put less focus on another aspect. The principle is so simple that many Americans forget about the priority difference between Chinese students and American students.

Without any doubts, Chinese teenagers today in general are a lot more driven in regard to education and pursuit of success. Please don't get me wrong. This statement is not absolute since there are still many American teenagers who work hard every day on education and the pursuit of monetary success. I am only making this statement in a general sense.

American teenagers are different than their counterparts in China on priorities. From my point of view, Americans place a lot more focus on personal happiness, family, love, and leisure. Such difference in priorities was very conspicuous as I was making the transition from China to North America.

As a ninth grader attending an American high school few years ago, I saw this distinction on priority. While I was in China, all we did was studying and doing homework. On most occasions, we had to study for tests coming up, especially the final exam. Through the school year, all we (Chinese teenagers) had to focus on was to study the school subjects carefully and to prepare for the final exam that would determine my future in the Chinese education system. Because of the intense pressure coming from the education system, my priority as a student was to study as hard as I can and to get as far as possible on my educational path.

For me, this was a huge priority because my father successfully went through college and used it to jumpstart his life. Aside from school, I did not know any other priorities in life. I was like a frog sitting in a well. I could only see a small piece of the sky, and I never was able to see anything more. I was trapped in the myopic world of education and success where education and hard work for success were the only priorities. The only other aspects of life in China were eating, sleeping, scarcely watching TV, and playing on a limited basis with friends with similar priorities.

When I moved to Canada as a sixth grader and to America as a ninth grader, I began to see this distinction between the priorities of North American children and Chinese children more clearly. In some interesting twists, I initially thought that American children at my school were crazy! I thought that they were planning to become street dwellers when they grow up! They were mostly indifferent of education and were very pessimistic about school. Quickly, I realized that was not the case, and there must be something different in America. There were simply too many of those people at my school with the same priorities. If that were true, all my fellow high school friends would be living on the street after high school!

The distinction was very conspicuous to me. American and Canadian students, instead of dedicating all of their lives to education and future monetary aspirations, are actually trying to enjoy life in the present through a variety of ways. They are trying to find boyfriends and girlfriends. They are attempting to seek love with courage. They are trying to be social and go to parties. They like to hang out with their friends on a consistent basis. They volunteer in their communities. They play sports and represent school teams. They go on vacations with their family. They play in bands and orchestras. They dance. They go on American Idol and try out. They sing at baseball games. They attend business conferences as teenagers. They help children with disabilities with the Best Buddies program.

In America, there are simply too many opportunities and attractions for students to pursue. That's one reason why the priorities for American teens are quite different. The priorities difference also comes hand in hand with the disparity on living standards between China and United States. American teenagers, on most occasions, have already experienced the good life. Even those who live in the lower half of American society still enjoy freedoms, ideals, opportunities, and benefits of this nation.

Because American students already realized the dreams that many Chinese students still want to realize, Americans tend to pursue other goals and set other priorities other than monetary success and luxuries of education. They have already come to believe that success and education are not everything in life. In some ways, Americans and the American way of thinking are more advanced than those of Chinese. Today, American students are striving to live a more fulfilling life while Chinese students are still hungry for what American students already take for granted.

Another explanation for the priority disparity may possibly be the family factor. In America, failing marriages that lead to divorces are extremely high. Many American children today are still experiencing the traumas of a broken family. Many of them may have already experienced the sudden departure of a father or a mother.

The family circumstance mainly affects the priority of American teenagers in two ways. On one hand, the teenager's priority changes for the better. Because he or she experienced the tragedies of a broken family and a failed marriage, he or she may place love and family unity at the top of his or her priority list instead of education and success. On the other hand, the priority can change in the complete opposite direction. A teenager may be deeply troubled by the broken family and drop education and future success as priorities in life. At this time, these teens have already lost hope for life and success.

Unlike America, China does not have a major issue with divorce and failing marriages based on percentage. Traditionally, such practice has been condemned by the general public. Even today, a divorce can look very bad on both the husband and the wife. Although there aren't major restrictions on divorce, Chinese still takes divorce very seriously and usually uses it as the very last option. Since divorce is not as common in China as it is in America, Chinese teenagers are not usually affected by divorce. This way, they are not inclined to change their priority on education and success like the American students.

In addition to divorce and priority change, there are significant differences between Americans and Chinese in general. Americans like to be more laid back and enjoy life day by day. Unlike them, the Chinese race was born to be more dedicated and more focused on education. As a Chinese myself, I can really understand the ways Chinese think—both young people and adults. We like to live for the future. When we are young, we like to study hard in order to attain a great career as adults. When we are adults, we like to earn as much money as possible and save them for the old age. This has been a cycle for centuries. For young people in China, the best way to shape a great and promising future is education. Through such perception, as a Chinese young person myself, I have already placed education as the highest priority in the earlier years of my life. I cannot help it because this has been a priority for the Chinese race for a long period of time.

While traditional differences such divorce rates and priorities based on tradition are some of the reasons, they are not the only reasons for the disparity on priorities. In many circumstances, these priorities can also be shaped by the American popular culture. My transition from China to America allowed me to see the drastic change in popular culture, which directly reflects my priorities in life.

When I used to live in China, I watched a lot of movies and TV shows. Maybe that's how I have become so nearsighted! Although there was a variety of movies and TV shows, I saw a very common theme. In almost all of the movies and TV shows I saw, they tend to glorify education and its abilities to change one's life dramatically. In many of these films, the main character was usually a country person or a person from a lower class. Eventually, this person rose into the middle class and the wealthy class simply by pursuing education in his earlier years.

In addition to the theme of education, the movies and TV shows there also promote the benefits and luxuries of the rich. In many movies, I can still remember how a person with wealth can always win over love and win the hearts of people. The lavish lifestyles of the wealthy delineated in those movies and TV shows truly seduced viewers to focus on education and to pursue wealth. Those themes captured the minds of the viewers such as me. When I saw those films and TV shows, I was influenced to believe that high education and personal wealth can enhance my happiness and bring loved ones to me.

American pop culture is very different. Its messages are more diverse. Instead of focusing on the joys of education and success, American movies show people, especially me, that there is more to life than a college degree and money. American entertainments focus more on the human characters and ideal ways to live life. I remembered watching *The Notebook*, which demonstrated how to love and to live a fulfilling life. I remembered *Forest Gump*, which inspired me to become a man who will follow my heart and accomplish in different aspects of life. I can still remember watching *Saving Private Ryan*, which allowed me to understand the importance of serving one's country and attaining positive morality facing challenges. Those are some of the lessons I learned from American pop culture. It truly opened my eyes to new themes and inspired me to go beyond education and monetary success. Despite many conservatives who have been criticizing the liberal nature of American pop culture, it has really helped me develop as a human being. It allowed me to reshape my priorities in life and take a more correct stance on personal happiness.

Pop culture can have significant influence on one's priority in life. I don't know for certain exactly how pop culture and the culture in general have affected the priorities in the lives of young people. However, I do know how it affected me on a personal level. As a person who was originally born in China and lived there for most of my life, I already firmly established my priorities in life before I moved here. I used to think that education at an elite college like Harvard and monetary success like that of Bill Gates would be my priorities and dreams in life. Those priorities altered after I moved to America. Because of the pop culture and the interaction with Americans, I realized that there's more to life than simply education and money.

Without a doubt, the Chinese will be more determined to become a better engineer, a better doctor, a better scientist, or a better inventor. There are no doubts because those are their goals and priorities in life. However, I would not be jealous or eager to attain similar priorities if I were an American. Although next generation's Chinese will be very intelligent and very competitive in all areas from a technical perspective, the Americans should still live a life with better ideals and better perceptions of the world. Such principles and priorities are priceless. Sometimes, those ideals bring true happiness and satisfaction.

Societal Disparity

Yin and Yang has been a part of the Chinese culture for the longest of times. According to the traditional Chinese philosophy, *Yin and Yang* is a phenomenon of two opposing forces in nature. Although the forces may seem to be extremely different and disjunctive, they are actually interdependent in the natural world. Outside the realm of Chinese philosophy, this idea is ironically an illustration of disparity between the Chinese and American society. Nowadays, because of this disparity in society, we have seen dramatic differences on the developments of young people. Chinese young people are more education and career-success inclined. Young Americans are more laid-back relatively in comparison.

One aspect that creates disparity between the two societies is the system of job distribution. I personally never had the opportunities to go through this system in China. However, I had personally seen my parents and family members go through a system in China that is very different from America's. This system has increased the cultural gap between China and America.

When I was a young child around the age of 6 years old, I lived with my grandparents. My grandfather always liked to tell stories about his youth and his accomplishments in life. Once, he told me that he graduated from a very prestigious college in China with an engineering degree. Because he graduated from one of the top universities in the nation in a very important scientific field, the government saw him as a rising star that would make contributions to the prospering nation. Therefore the government assigned him to a job in a research institution within a nationally-owned steel company in northern China. From this job, my grandfather was automatically launched into society as one of the middle-class.

This was a great leap for him. The government's system of job distribution, based on my grandfather's education backgrounds, allowed my grandfather to have the greatest break of his life. Prior to the assigned job, my grandfather had a very humble beginning. My grandfather lived in the rural region of China as a child. The region he lived in was one of the most impoverished areas in China. Almost few people were able to escape from the endless cycle of poverty. The only way for them to succeed was to excel in education. And that was exactly what my grandfather accomplished.

From the very beginning, my grandfather knew how the Chinese society worked. He understood that the government would automatically assign him great jobs if he were able to attain extremely high degrees in top universities. Such system in the Chinese society inspired my grandfather to gain a resolve to succeed in his education through hard works and complete dedication. In many ways, the society limited my grandfather to the path of education and continues to do so in today's society.

My grandfather was a success story in the Chinese system of education and distribution of jobs. However, I have also seen many failures as a young child. One of such failures was my uncle. My uncle was a smart and creative man. He had great ambitions and dreams in life. To certain extent, he could be as intelligent as my grandfather in many aspects of life. He has been very handy and very social in life. He has so many friends that he would have 4000 friends on Facebook if he would ever get one! However, he today is only a store employee. He still lives with my grandparents in a small apartment along with his wife and son. Even today, he does not have enough money to move out and buy an apartment of his own.

His fate was determined long ago when he was a young adult. As a teenager, he never applied himself in studying and education. In some ways, he was like many of my American friends. Like my American friends, he felt that he was smart enough to get by with mediocre efforts at school and mediocre grades. He always believed that life was too short to not live. Instead of dedicating his times to education like my grandfather, my uncle always hanged out with his friends on school nights and weekends.

While many American young people can fortunately get by with such behaviors and mentalities, my uncle lived in the Chinese society, and he faced his punishments later in life. Since my uncle and my grandfather are similar in hereditary traits, their footsteps in life should have been side by side. Yet the path they went through eventually diverged, and the destinations are very different today.

My grandfather attended a respectable university after his senior year in high school because of his outstanding academic achievements following hard works. In similar manner, he used the same work ethic and mentality in university and on his job at a research institution. His achievements and dedications allowed my family to have a more luxurious life today.

In contrast, my uncle barely made through high school and only attended a community college. In China, the government has a lot of authority over the distribution of jobs, and it always gives good jobs to highly educated individuals. Due to this kind of control, people like my uncle who are inherently smart but lack in education have no chance in moving up in society. They don't even have opportunities to start their own businesses and to make up their lack of formal education with creativity. In China, those opportunities are usually given to the educated individuals through government and universities.

My uncle is trapped. His weaknesses in lack of education and degrees have cornered his life into a dead end. This is a pattern that has repeated countless times among the preceding Chinese generations. Those mistakes have been publicized in the Chinese education systems, and many young Chinese today have observed the tragic endings to people who did not take education seriously. Today, most young Chinese have already learned from those mistakes and realized that they need to attain better education in order to have a shot at the good life. That's the reason why Chinese young people in general are more dedicated to education compared to young Americans.

Since I moved to North America, especially United States, I made a very interesting observation. In America, many high school students prefer technical schools and trainings over traditional academic education. Instead of learning the philosophical side of chemistry, biology, mathematics, and physics, a lot of young Americans think that applied education through technical schools and career centers is more helpful in life. And they are right! This is quite true in North America. People who attend those schools sometimes can have better incomes than those who attend traditional universities.

At my high school, there is a career center beside the high school campus. Many of my friends at school take both academic courses and technical courses at the career center. Through the early introduction of technical training, many young Americans go directly to technical schools and pursue careers as mechanics, chefs, police, etc. Many times, those careers offer higher salaries compared to the jobs for university graduates. Because of this circumstance, a lot of American students put less focus on traditional education and pursue technical training. This situation directly contributes to the declining of American education standards at academic schools and universities.

I remember the times when I was swimming and exercising at a local sports facility. When I was there, I met a very interesting man. To me, he is the paragon of the everyday American who took his children to the facility to have fun on a weekend afternoon. While I was exercising, I got to have chats with him, and I learned a lot through those chats. During our conversations, he soon found out that I was a senior in high school, and he offered some advice. To my surprise, instead of telling me that I need to study harder in my senior year like all the Chinese adults, he told me that education was a joke, and it would be useless in life.

What!? That was exactly what my mind was thinking when he uttered those advice. As an inquisitive person, I asked him to elaborate on his point of view. As a result, he told me that, in his opinion, what people learn in school like Calculus, general mathematics, and chemistry is useless. As a college dropout, he told me that most jobs in American do not require those skills. To him, he wasted three years in college studying engineering, and then he dropped out. The man told me that in life, what is learned in school would most often be obsolete. He provided an example. He claimed that he worked at a high tech firm. At his workplace, he earned a lot more money than his PhD friends, and he did not even finish college.

As we continued to carry on the discussion, I listened patiently. It was a very revealing dialogue because I was able to analyze the mindset of a typical American. He represents a great number of people living in the United States. I can absolutely guarantee that his mindsets on education and school are very similar to a majority of Americans today. With such state of mind, today's reality in America is not as surprising as we might originally think.

Unlike America, China is a nation that solely adopts traditional education. If I were to attend technical schools instead of traditional universities, I would have careers in general with low salaries. A great example to this reality is my aunt Ying.

My aunt Ying travelled a different path from my grandfather's in education. She was one of those students who never worked hard enough at school and failed to attain high grades that are necessary for Chinese universities. In many ways, I can even compare the work ethics of my aunt Ying in school with the work ethics of many young American students today. Because of her inability to attend a traditional four-year university, she attended a special three-year teacher's college. While in America, a teacher can usually attain a better career than most university graduates—even if they attended a three-year college. This is not the same for China.

Following graduation, my aunt Ying became a middle school teacher. In the United States, a middle school teacher is relatively well-respected and well-paid. In China, that was not the case for my aunt. While my grandfather entered society as a middle-class, my aunt did not. She was not paid well as a teacher, and she had to work long hours. Because of her technical degree from a teacher's college, her income was not very high. Even her job as a middle school geography teacher did not earn her much respects among her peers. This was all the results of her technical school background instead of a traditional university.

China is a country that looks highly at university degrees. Many times, higher degrees in college result in higher respects in a career field. Respects in China lead to higher salaries and higher status in society. A PhD's degree would usually earn better income than a Master's Degree. A Master's Degree would earn higher income than a Bachelor's Degree.

This is completely different in America. In America, companies prefer experiences and practical trainings over degrees. That's why a technician in America can sometimes earn more salaries than a company certified researcher. Although this is not most often true, this is most definitely a huge possibility.

I can still recall times when my uncle Wang had to apply for jobs when he first moved to Canada. He immigrated a year after my family moved to Canada. At the time, my uncle had a Chinese mentality. He thought that by listing his Master's and PhD's Degrees, he would have a better chance to find a job. However, he was very wrong. He was rejected many times because the companies thought his education background was too deep and lacks actual technical experience. Sometimes, the companies in America are also threatened by extremely high degrees. They prefer people with real abilities instead of just academic success. With this type of situation, American young people don't have to really work hard to attain higher degrees while Chinese students do.

In addition to differences on the importance of traditional education, the very definition of success has been muttered in the pot of Chinese and American. In China, the general perception of success has been very materialistic. Even though I am not saying this for everyone, this has been a very fascinating trend I have observed.

I am speaking from experience. My grandparents who represent the average class of Chinese should be great models for most Chinese people. Since I was a young child, my grandmother and grandfather defined success for me without my own research, and such message has been deeply inked in my mind after years of reiterations.

My grandmother, on one hand, has always told me that the only way I can live a happy and respectful life is with wealth from a monetary point of view. Although she never directly told me that money is everything and can buy me everything in this world, I can sense that she wants me to have a lot of money in order to avoid tough times like she and my grandfather did. My grandfather, on the other hand, always reminds me that I came from a very humble root. He constantly talked about my family (including my relatives in China) and how they all count me to make a lot of money and be successful. He wants me to bring honor to the Zhao family and finally erase years of failures, poverties, and disappointments.

Of course, as a young child, I asked my parents and grandparents how I would ever make a lot of money and be "successful". Throughout the years, I have always received the same answer: "You need to stay in school and make good grades. You need high test scores. You need to study. This way you can get into an elite university. Those graduates will always become extremely wealthy." In similar manners, my parents' friends and relatives taught the same definition and ideology to their children. I am quite certain that the same definition has been transferred from parents to children in many households in China.

Through my early lessons on "success" from my family, I always believed that great education and a plethora of money are the only ways for me to be successful. This perception never changed or altered until I moved to America and attended an American school.

In America, I learned a completely new definition of success. I realized that becoming successful and achieving the American dream never requires me to have an elite education and high net worth. I found that there is more to success. I finally saw its complexity and breadth through my eye opening experience in America.

Although money and education are factors to success, Americans taught me that there are more to success than just money and education. While a person can be rich with money, he or she can also be rich with friends, family, love, passion, compassion, and courage. This lesson has been extremely valuable to me.

When I used to live in Vancouver, Canada, I made a great friend named Derek. He lived next door to my rented house, and we always hanged out. It was the toughest yet also the happiest time of my life.

I was a new immigrant and did not know any English. I was very lost and confused about my circumstance and my future. Additionally, I made a great friend who was patient enough with my language barriers, and we had a blast playing together.

One aspect that stood out to me when I first met him was that he and his family were very happy. I was initially very confused. I always thought that money and education were the only factors leading to success and happiness. And Derek's family did not match any of the two factors for success. Both his parents were only high school graduates. They never attended a day of school in college. They did not have any technical training. Both his parents worked as workers and laborers. His father actually had three different jobs and had to work on all seven days. According to my family's standards, they were failures in life. However, they were wrong.

When I asked Derek's parents how they felt about their lives, they answered quickly and confidently. They said: "We love our lives together as a family. We enjoy spending times together during the very limited amount of free time we have. We are satisfied with our daily works. We think that it's great to have busy and fulfilling days. While we don't earn a lot of money, the money we do earn is honest and joyful! We are quite successful from the perspective of living life."

After hearing their answers, I was emotionally moved. My belief on success slowly changed. Their mentality and their fulfilling lives as average people have made them successful. I saw how happy they were. On the contrary, I saw rich Americans who had to deal with controversies and broken families. At that point, my thinking was forever altered. While this experience was one of many lessons I learned about success, this was the most monumental one in my life. It opened up the door for me to truly understand Americans. This also enabled me to see a clear disparity between Chinese and American society.

At one end of world, Chinese people think that money and education are the only determinants to success. This made young Chinese to push themselves to work harder academically. Through excessive hard work and dedication on education, the Chinese education system has produced many extremely bright and talented individuals who mostly are better than their competitors in America on a technical basis.

At the other end of the world, young Americans have a different and broader view of success. This enabled them to pursue many aspects of life other than education and money. Although today's Americans do not have the outstanding academic and technical skills like those of Chinese students, they have a more sophisticated and wholesome mentality. Sometimes, such mentality is very important on a person's success. Because of this reality, there is actually a balance between the competitive edge of Chinese and American students in the future—one has great abilities and one has great mentalities.

TWELVE

Technology Seduction

"Technology is so much fun but we can drown in our technology. The fog of information can drive out knowledge." American social historian and educator Daniel J. Boorstin iterated this gleaming quote. What's more impressive about Mr. Boorstin is that he uttered the adage in 1914, and yet the truth to his saying has never been truer than it is today. Ironically, the social historian's posterities, young Americans, who he originally addressed to, are the epitomes of his foreboding warning.

If you still think that technologies have nothing to do with the academic achievements and determinations of American students today, you are still very much in denial. From my experiences and observations, technologies do not play a little role in the academic achievements and development disparity between young Chinese students and young American students. They play a critical role.

Ever since I moved to America from China, I transitioned from limited consumer electronics in my life to an abundance of them. Of course, I have since become a victim of technology similar to my American comrades. Like the quote iterated, I was drowned in a sea of technological distractions, and my academic propensity as well as love for studying waned. Today, I have to honestly admit that my academic standard and skills have fallen very far behind my counterparts in China. Even though I rank number one in my graduating class in the status quo, I am still quite far from Chinese students of my age in advancement of mathematics, science, language, technologies, philosophy, etc. Technology has been a huge factor to this reality.

In the United States, affordable consumer electronics and high salaries comparable to other countries allow many of us to purchase many consumer technologies. There are iPods, countless brands of computers and laptops, gaming systems, comprehensive selection of cell phones, video players, high definition televisions, and many more.

In addition to the available and affordable technologies, infrastructures in support of those technologies such as satellites, cable, high speed internet, and wireless network are firmly established throughout the nation. Nowadays, because of existing infrastructures in America, young Americans have taken for granted the easy access to technologies. Using them is very simple and convenient.

Technologies are everywhere in American households, and the young people have been heavily lured by those wonderful and exciting technologies. Even for a teenager with Chinese blood and values, I have not been able to resist those kinds of seductions coming from technologies. I have been struggling with the hook of technologies, and they have continued to decrease my interests in studying and academic endeavors.

For the first half of my young life, I lived in China with my parents, my grandparents, and many relatives. While I was living there, technologies certainly existed. There were gaming systems, computers, music players, games, and many other consumer technologies. However, I as a student was never affected by them. My indifference to technologies at the time was not the result of my personal restrain. It was mainly a lack of access for me as a child.

Consumer electronics in China was not very affordable for the common folks. Usually, a common household can only afford one or two of those technologies. The unaffordability was a two-way streak. In the first place, the average salaries for households were commonly quite low. Many people simply did not have enough budgets to purchase such luxuries. Furthermore, the prices of those technologies were very expensive. Many Americans would probably think otherwise since most of such technologies are made in China. However, those consumer electronics are directly shipped to America for profit. Then American companies import them back to Chinese market for higher prices. On many occasions, they are more expensive than they are in America.

Coupled with those challenges, the Chinese culture promotes many values, and they are usually enforced by adults onto their children. One of such values was to use less technologies and consumer electronics. Chinese families, especially elders, usually prevent children like me from using them because they hold a belief that technologies such as HDTV, gaming systems, and computers could corrupt young people. From a physical health perspective, they believe that excessive use of those technologies can really hurt young people's eyes and make them very nearsighted. Nearsightedness is not a very common problem among Americans due to cultural hereditary disparity. However, it is very serious in China. From a mental health perspective, they generally feel that technologies can corrupt young minds and influence indecent and profane behaviors.

When I was young living in China, technologies were not very common then because the nation was just recently opened up to the western society. And high consumer technologies were mainly western. Only recently did consumer technologies' understandings and popularities rise in China. Comparatively, they do not have as strong an influence on China as they have on America, especially on young people. China is still playing catch-up to western civilizations on technologies. They still do not rely on technologies as much as Americans do.

Since I was raised in that society until I was 10 years old, I got used to living without any consumer technologies such as gaming systems and cell phones. They were simply too expensive to buy, especially for a young kid like me. The wireless networks for cell phones and internets for computers were very inconvenient at the time. Even if I were able to purchase the items, I would not be able to afford the service charges.

Even if my family could afford it, they would never allow me to use them. Because technologies were such delicacies in China, adults like parents would never trust me with cell phones, computers, or music players. Because of such harsh reality, I was limited to only television and cassette player. Such limited choices in technologies in that part of my life gave me more time for academic works and studying in general that would prepare me for my future. I was rarely overwhelmed with the technological lure like I have to face today.

Television had a very specific schedule in China, and I only watched it on few occasions of the day. Cassette players required many batteries and music cassettes. Those aspects acted as limiting factors to my time using the music player and allowed me to use more time for useful tasks.

For me, the only option was studying and school work. Even if I completed my school assignments, I wanted to learn more and go above and beyond the curriculum because there were no major distractions preventing me from doing so. That's also partly the reason why Chinese students are more skilled academically and prepared for international competition compared to American students. Because they don't have many distractions, they do not have to balance time spending with electronics and time spending on studying. They have more time for education and usually go above and beyond the "already very high" academic requirements at school.

Such circumstances never occurred after my move. I was overwhelmed by a sea of electronics and technologies as I moved to Canada and United States. Because of a better standard of living and more opportunities to purchase new electronics, I was able to attain many entertainments such as iPod Touch, HDTV, laptop, gaming systems, Smartphone, and portable DVD player.

In addition to the electronics, my family was able to afford high speed internet, wireless network for cell phones, and cable. In the past as a Chinese student, I enjoyed reading books and studying new subjects in the world of academia. The reason I did that was not because I naturally love doing them. The reason was that I was bored, and there were not many gadgets I could play with. This completely changed in America.

With my laptop and the high speed internet connection, I spend most of my free times during the day on the computer and on the internet. There are simply too much to do on the computer. I can play games on my laptop, either online or offline. I can do some shopping online, which can take up to hours. I can watch movies, videos, and TV shows on my computer. Sometimes, I can download a whole season of a television show and watches it for hours without stopping. Now, social networking is huge in United States. With Facebook, Myspace, and Twitter, I can spend hours of my day looking at other people's profiles and chatting with friends. When I combine my time playing computer games, watching TV shows and movies, social networking, and shopping online, the time spent on those activities can accumulate into countless hours. I usually use entire weekends and after school times on the computer and on the internet when I don't hang out with my friends.

This distraction has taken away tremendous amount of time from my studying and academic pursuits that would better prepare me for the future. The computer and the internet are simply too seductive for me. I cannot resist it. Even when I was determined to do my homework and to do some extra studying, I always end up thinking that I can just play the computer for 20 minutes and actually play for hours. This rarely happened to me when I was in China because we could not afford computers, and the internet service was extremely expensive. Today, Chinese teenagers are facing similar kind of addictions, though the addictions for them are not as severe. However, a large number of Chinese students still do not have access to technologies like laptops and internets, and they still have opportunities to focus on studying and future preparation.

To make the matters worse, there are more electronics other than computers. There are still iPods and cell phones. While television and computers dominate the lives of many young Americans at home, iPods and cell phones disrupt young Americans at school. As a Chinese-born teenager, I never really had any trouble with iPods and cell phone distractions at school. Mainly, it's the result of my parents who always check what I bring to school. If I do bring iPod to school, I would usually be reprimanded. For example, I have both an iPod Nano and an iPod Touch. However, my parents always hide them during school days, thus I don't bring them to school.

Likewise, they also control my cell phone usage at school. Although they allow me to bring my cell phone to school unlike my iPods, they refuse to install a texting plan on my cell phone. This way, I would not be able to text in class while the teacher is teaching. Texting is the most dangerous feature of cell phones, and it can severely affect my education at school. My parents know that I would never be able to talk on the cell phone in class since the teachers are going to see me committing such action. Thus texting is the only threat, and they have eliminated it.

Unlike me, American young adults do not have similar controls from their parents. From my experience with my American friends and peers, their parents are more laid-back compared to the Chinese parents. They trust their children more and provide them freedoms so the children can make their own decisions.

I don't want to sound negative, but such approach has failed. While there are certain American young people who innately have great self-control and personal ambitions in life, most of them are not. But who can blame them. They are just kids, and they can always make poor choices. With the freedom they attain, most American young people abuse them.

Since many American students have texting as a feature on their cell phone plan, they use them at school on a consistent basis. I never had the opportunities to have the texting plan, and I never really personally experienced with texting in class while the teacher was teaching. However, I had seen enough to know how it's affecting the academic results of American students. And I was irritated to see American students who text in class and completely disregard their education.

No matter if it's regular English class or Advanced Placement English class, American students always text while the instructor is teaching something important. Sure, many of them still take notes from the board. But, they are not thinking while taking notes. They are not really taking in and absorbing the material. We all know that multitasking is a myth. No one can do two things at once with the same quality as doing one thing at once. Because they are texting, my American friends are not fully attempting to learn the material necessary for academic success. In similar manner, they are not preparing themselves for international competition.

Many American students are only engaged on the conversation through their cell phones. They are not actually placing their focuses on the academic material. It's very frustrating for me to see. It feels like that they are wasting their opportunities at school. They are wasting the chance to attend school for free and to prepare them for their futures. I know tons of students in China who can only hope to attend a school but cannot afford to.

I understand that having a cell phone in class with texting is very alluring. If I were to have the same privilege, I would probably unable to control myself either like I do with computers. And that's why I think American students are not the ones to be blamed for falling behind in preparation for global competition. It's the options of having technologies and electronics that created the gap on academic dedication and quality.

In some ways, the wealth of America and its growing consumer electronic industry have been the villains in this chapter of American educational fallout. They are the ones who have superfluously produced appealing technologies and pull young Americans behind on international competition. Additionally, American parents are also responsible. If they were to enforce stricter rules and to limit the availability of such technologies to their children, we may have a different story today. Nevertheless, I have to admit that with all the distractions from technologies and electronics in American students' lives, the abilities of many American students to hang on are quite impressive and worth applauding.

To be fairly honest, the American educational curriculum, especially in high school, is somewhat easier than that of China. By combining an easier curriculum with less dedicated students, the result, without any doubts, is today's difference between China and United States on academic excellence and quality of students. From history, one lesson we have consistently learned is that wealth and prosperity usually bring contentment and unforeseen disadvantages. Today's American society is the epitome of such axiom. Because of America's prosperity on many fronts such as technologies and consumer electronics, it has corrupted its posterities in education and in competition with other students from other nations. This is an unforeseen disadvantage.

In similar manner, an austere lifestyle and a lack of prosperity can sometimes bring new advantages. This is why Chinese students have thrived academically and in career preparation. Sometimes, we cannot do anything to change the force of nature. In the cycle of nature, there is always a cycle of rise, height, and decline. Unfortunately, America has already reached its height and is facing a new wave of decline. In the contrary, China, because of its young class of talented individuals in different fields, is on the rise from its past low.

Right now, the only question is how can America maintain its height and decrease the rate of decline. One way is to control the distractions of technologies on young Americans and to wake up from a bad hangover due to prosperity. In other words, young Americans need to be reintroduced to hard work academically and determination for the future career. It's only through this route Americans can be once again competitive facing global competition.

Teenage Love in the Air

Have you seen a movie before? Most likely, the answer would be "yes". If you have seen movies before, you must have realized that the theme of love has been a usual topic. No matter where you live (China, India, Korea, United States, etc), there are movies about love on a consistent basis. For some reasons, romantic movies have been huge hits and are money generating machines world-wide.

From those movies, there has always been one common plot. In the beginning, a man and a woman live two separate lives filled with work, education, success, and ambitions. Then they meet and fall in love. In the end, they have to give up their original ambitions in career and education for love. Such plot is almost predictable to the movie goers. Of course, the movies are most often fictional. However, the effects of love on a person's life are 100 percent factual.

Throughout history, both love and infatuation have been the most powerful factors in altering one's life.

Love's effects were proven even at the inception of humanity. Of course, many of you probably know Adam and Eve, either from common knowledge or biblical study. Adam was the first man created, and he was loved by his creator. Then Eve came along and was tricked by a serpent to eat the supposedly poisonous apple. Although Adam knew it was going to be a terrible idea, his love for Eve was stronger than his common sense and judgment. Because of his love, he did not restrain Eve from consuming the apple their creator warned them not to eat, and the rest of the story has been history.

The same idea applies to young people from across the world. This has been partially the reason why Chinese students are more driven and focused on their education in relationship to young Americans. In turn, Chinese young people are more prepared for globalization.

To be very clear, China was founded on the foundation of social conservatism. This foundation has been the reason why Chinese people are so keen and determined to keep their great traditions as a nation. In contrast, America is a country founded on social conservatism, but it has emerged into a society of social liberalism. While America is still on the center-right of the political spectrum (moderate to conservative), the social aspect has always been quite liberal. At least since I moved to America! That's why Americans usually are introduced to the idea of love at a very young age, and this idea has prevented young Americans from focusing on education and future career success.

I quickly learned that when I first attended middle school in Canada. Then the same situation repeated since I moved to United States for high school. Every day, as I walk in the hallways of my American high school, I can see girls and boys holding hands. Some of them even go to the extreme and display their affections for each other in public.

Initially, I was shocked by the openness and casualness of teenagers who go around as couples. I only saw that in more mature institutions such as college and shopping mall in China. After initial reactions, I went through a period of nausea when I observe those occurrences. I wanted to gag when young Americans, even middle school students and freshmen, kiss in the hall and publicly announce their affections. Is this even legal? That was a question revolving in my mind for awhile. I was confused, shocked, and sick all at the same time. I was not used to this type of situation in China. The feeling I had was as if I saw a talking dog! That's how shocking it was for me. Eventually, I went pass the awkward initial stage, and I now am used to such situations in school.

The concept of dating and having girlfriends and boyfriends in middle and high school was almost nonexistent when I was a kid in China. Maybe today's China has somewhat loosened up in that concept, but it's definitely not as severe as it is in American schools. Additionally, unlike Americans, those behaviors in middle and high school are heavily condemned by the population and the community—even in a modern Chinese society.

Of course, many of you are wondering why wouldn't young Chinese students go out and find girlfriends and boyfriends? There are simply too many reasons. First and foremost, the precedence for such behavior is very important. In North America, such acts are quite normal for middle school and high school students. When American teenagers arrive at that age, they will want to follow the precedents of the past American teenagers. Many times, the teenagers' parents did the same when they were young. Some of the young Americans are even the products of young love in high school.

In China, there is generally no precedence. China, for a long period of time, was a backward nation. Because of the past backwardness, the precedence of young students having girlfriends and boyfriends is nonexistent. Since there was generally no precedence of such occurrences in China, Chinese middle and high school students don't generally go out on dates. Such ideas are simply strangers to their minds. Their parents, most likely, never had such relationships when they were in middle school and high school. For Chinese young people, dating at a young age is like walking into a dark room without knowing what is ahead.

In addition to precedence, the foundation and ideals of the society is another explanation. China is a socially conservative nation. If you don't know about this fact, you should evaluate the management of money in China as an example. In China, people don't go out and waste their money. They actually invest a lot of their money or save them in banks. In America, on the other hand, people do like to spend money on luxuries and don't usually like to save money. Because of the dissimilarity on the management of money, we can clearly see that China is a more socially conservative nation.

Because of the social conservatism, China has a class of very socially conservative adults and parents. Unlike generally more liberal American parents, Chinese parents put a lot of focus on the more conservative developments of their children. The idea of having boyfriends and girlfriends in middle school and high school is almost always unacceptable to most Chinese parents. While Americans may think this is cute, Chinese parents think it's unhealthy.

If you are not yet convinced, we should take a look at the teenage pregnancy statistics. Teenage pregnancy can help us explore the effects of dating at a young age. In United States, statistic is almost shocking. Nowadays, just under 1/3 of all teenage girls in America are pregnant. Around 750,000 young people will get pregnant in the United States per year. As a result, 2/3 of those students do not complete high school and usually move onto a path of anguish and struggles as adults. United States has been known as the country with the highest teenage pregnancy rates in civilized world. Undoubtedly, it's the result of early age dating and falling in love. Conversely, China's statistic is almost flawless and negligent up to now.

The most straightforward reason for those contrasts in statistics is the control of the parents and the makeup of the society. I can still remember times when I was a kid. My family liked to watch television and movies, and we only had one television set. As a result, we had to watch TV together. When we were watching movies and TV shows, there were occasionally kissing scenes in them. My parents, the typical socially conservative Chinese parents, told me to turn around immediately. This type of restrictions lasted until middle school. However, my parents still occasionally do that after I have become a high school student. That's how conservative Chinese parents can be. They put focus on every little detail like preventing children from watching a little kissing scene on television.

With the parents looking behind Chinese young people's backs, the Chinese pop culture adds an additional push against teenage relationships. When I mention "Chinese" pop culture, it is quite different from "American" pop culture. In China, TV shows and movies tend to promote love and relationship in a more sacred manner. They always dramatize relationship between a man and a woman and make it very complicated. Sometimes, the main character would find his or her true love after years of misunderstandings and grief. This type of pop culture influence not only drives teens away from relationship, but it also creates a very misleading atmosphere. Sometimes, teenagers in China idealize love and relationship too much after those cultural influences that they often fear having a relationship early in their lives.

On the other hand, American pop culture is completely the opposite. Almost all television shows and movies with the involvement of young people express a side of teenage relationships and love conflict. Even in Disney shows that have mostly young viewers around age 8 to 12, the plot of falling in love with a boy or girl at school and starting a relationship has been very common. Shows on Disney such as *Hannah Montana* and *Suite Life of Zack and Cody* all have plots related to young kids going out and getting girlfriends and boyfriends. Many times, this type of pop culture influence affects behaviors of children and students at school. That's why American students usually jump into a romantic relationship at a very young age.

So what's wrong with having girlfriends and boyfriends? Isn't this a good thing? Isn't it cute when this happens? To be honest, there is nothing wrong with entering a relationship as middle and high school students. I learned that this is a very important social experience in American society, and this is part of the American culture. And yes, it is very cute when a young boy and a young girl go on dates and act as little adults. However, this reality has partially led to the disparity between American students and Chinese students in the area of education. While Chinese young people focus on future preparation for global competition, American young people are often distracted by teenage relationships.

Many Americans today are anxious because young Chinese students are excelling in areas such as science, technology, mathematics, etc. They are extremely competitive facing global competition, and they are planning to take jobs away from the American students because of their abilities in those fields. One reason that Chinese students are able to do better in those academic fields is because they have time and less distractions away from academic studies. While American students are preoccupied with relationships and love, Chinese students are limited to studying because of the conservative social nature of the society, their parents, and their shy temperament facing the opposite sex.

It's good to have love and relationship, but they do take a lot of time. American students in relationships often have to sacrifice their dedications to education. They have to make time to go on dates. They have to have free time for spending time with their boyfriends and girlfriends. They have to experience emotional rollercoaster while making their relationship work. Often they also have to fulfill many social obligations. All these aspects of young relationships are like powerful vacuums taking away precious times that could have spent on education.

In life, no one can have everything. In our circumstance, the Chinese students sacrificed relationships and young loves—mainly because of circumstantial factors—for education, and the American students sacrificed in-depth education on many levels for love and relationships. One ends up as a long term investment while the other works as a whim of joy and pleasure.

Sometimes, the differences between societies are too great— just like China and America. We can never blame the young people. We cannot blame the Chinese students on their lack of love and social life. It's not because Chinese students don't want to have them. On most occasions, the Chinese society's values, priorities, and culture block them from making those choices.

Likewise, we cannot blame American students for having too much social life and sacrificing future preparation in the form of education. The American society has been very liberal, and the general cultural trend acts as peer pressure to drive American young people to all those social activities such as having a boyfriend or girlfriend.

In many respects, both Chinese and American young people started together on the same starting line. However, their roads diverged because of external factors. Somehow, the wind of societal difference has pushed them onto different paths in different directions. This diverging road has led us to today's reality. On one hand, we have the American young people who have to juggle everything from social activities to relationships. On the other hand, we have the Chinese young people who have only one goal in mind—education and career success (maybe also beating American students through global competition).

FOURTEEN

No Chance vs. Vast Opportunities

Option is the single most important driver in a person's life. It's not wealth. It's not intelligence. It's not how cool a person is or how hot a person is. It is option. In today's society, I found that "option" has been the most clichéd and overused word. Due to the trite uses of the word "option", its supposedly straight forward definition has been muttered up. Likewise, its importance has been downplayed in many circumstances. Yet option has been one of the most important factors that have dramatically differentiated American students from Chinese students. And because of this differentiation, we have seen two very different approaches to education and life.

If American parents want to lay blames on those who made American children fall behind in education, they should definitely blame all the options and opportunities that exist in the American society and its education system. It's kind of ironic, but it's very true. Ever since I moved to America from China, I experienced this drastic shift in the amount of opportunities and options in life and in the education system. This drastic shift has altered my perception on traditional education and reordered my priorities in life.

Although it has been six years since I last attended a Chinese school and lived in the Chinese society, my memories there are still deeply locked within my mind. One of the most vivid memories I have is the lack of options for young people in China. Don't get me wrong. China is a nation filled with fresh opportunities, especially following the economic boom in recent years. However, what I am pointing out is that Chinese society and its education system do not offer many opportunities and option to its young people in general.

When I was an elementary student back in Anshan, an industrial city in northern China, I rarely had anything to do other than school works, school lectures, sleeping, hanging out with friends, spending time with family, and regular entertainments (TV, Internet, etc). This lack of options in life as a student caused me to put a lot more focus and dedication on education and future career success in a selected field.

At school, the only activities we had were recess, teacher lectures, and lunch. This is quite different compared to American elementary schools. Although elementary schools are more laid-back, American elementary schools sometimes have student government and leisure clubs other than classes and school works. Additionally, American communities offer a lot of activities and opportunities for young people out of school. Unfortunately, Chinese young people don't have the same options.

I am pretty sure that many of you are still skeptical about my experience in school and perceptions of Chinese schools' lack of extracurricular opportunities for students. Much of skepticism may come from the fact that I was only an elementary student. Even in

America, elementary school students don't have many extracurricular activities. That's why I am also going to bring up some of my family members in China and their experiences in Chinese high schools.

My cousin Fan was a high school student before I moved to America. More specifically, he was in his third year of high school. Throughout the years, we have been very good friends. We liked to hang out together because he was extremely cool and wise, and I was very funny and innocent. He liked to tease me because I was so confused about the common senses of the world. I also had very funny looking teeth with gigantic gaps! He often joked about them. While we were hanging out together, I got to know a lot about his school life as a Chinese high school student.

He always complained about the amount of pressure he had with education and earning good grades at school. He was tired of the system because he believed it was dull and limited in opportunities. To him, his life as a high school student consisted of 10 hours of school each day and many more hours of extra studying outside. But don't get fooled with the long hours of school. Those 10 hours did not include any extracurricular activities. It was hardcore learning in mathematics, science, Chinese, English, and social studies.

He constantly talked about attempting to escape from the system and do something else as a young person. However, he honestly did not know what to do. There were simply too few options. Even after 10 hours of school and many hours of studying, he still had some free time. During those free times, many Americans would probably choose one of many options that exist for students. But he could not. The only option he had was sleeping and extra tutoring on school work.

While I lived in China, I also saw high school there through the eyes of a high school educator. My aunt Shu Bin was a high school teacher, and she knew a lot about Chinese students. She has worked with them ever since she left teachers' college. Because she and my mother were great friends ever since college, I had many opportunities to spend time with her. I can almost recall the time when she almost adopted me as her godson. That's how close she was with my family.

During our times together, I can always remember what she said. She always had a lot of stories about her days dealing with Chinese students. She also had a lot to say about the Chinese education system. One day, my mother, my aunt Shu, and I went to a local KFC restaurant. My mother just came home from southern China, and she had not seen her best friend, my aunt Shu, for a year. As a side note, KFC restaurant was actually a delicacy in China. It was not like the fast food restaurant Americans think about. It was foreign and very expensive in China.

While we were there, my aunt Shu started to talk with my mother, and I ease dropped. She was talking about me and my future in China. My aunt Shu worried for me. As a high school teacher, she shared the pains of her students every day. She told my mother that she envied children in other countries. Although she was a great teacher, she felt that the system for education in China forced students to only focus on education. The force was not actually enforced with laws. It was enacted because of the lack of activities and options for students. She recalled that all her students did every day were studying.

As a high school teacher, she was fortunate to earn a lot of income. However, most of the salary did not come through the education system. The majority of those incomes came from tutoring students outside of school. In China, the only options and activities students had after school were more tutoring on the school subjects. This is especially true for students in higher grades such as high school students. Extra tutoring was the only type of activities the school system had to offer to the students. Such activity not only prevented students from exploring other aspects of life, but it also added more emphasis to education in the minds of the Chinese young people.

In direct contrast to the realities that exist in China, American society itself and the education system have given their young people so many options and opportunities outside of school. My high school experience in the United States is the proof to such statement of contrast.

When my father found a job in the United States at the end of my middle school years, my parents and I moved to the heartland of United States. We actually moved to Midwestern United States—Indiana to be more specific. There was almost no where better than Indiana to represent the true nature of America and the American spirit. In order to have a real American experience, we moved to a small town, and I attended a local city high school. At this local city school and community, I finally realized exactly how many options I have as a young person. Those are the teenage opportunities that I never had in China, and they are the same opportunities many of my Chinese friends and families dreamed of.

It's not like I attended a model high school in the United States. As a matter of fact, the high school I attended was blue-collar and below-average in relationship to many high schools in the United States. The majority of students' parents were workers at a local car manufacturing plant. Despite the subpar standard of living and below-average high school, I found so many options and opportunities as a student there. I never would imagine them if I continued to live in China.

One of the most conspicuous options for American students is athletics teams at school. In China, athletics was only recreational for high school students. Average Chinese high school students don't have the opportunities to play on a real athletics team at the high school. If one wanted to play sports on a team and explore his or her talents, one in China had to enroll in a special athletics training school supported by the government. This meant giving up in his or her academic career and place complete dedication on athletics. Thus normal high school students in China do not have options to play team sports and compete with other schools.

In America, the system is different. High schools offer many athletics teams for students to join. There are basketball teams, soccer teams, football teams, baseball teams, track teams, swimming teams, and wrestling teams. In wealthier schools, there are also lacrosse teams, hockey teams, golf teams, tennis teams, and sailing teams. Because there are so many sports teams, students with enough talents and loves for the sports can actually experience opportunities to play the sports on a competitive level. Many times, students who play sports at school can realize that they have enough skills and talents to excel in the sports and maybe one day become a professional.

Through the opportunities to play on a sports team, American students may place less focus on education and use a lot of time to get better in a specific sport. As a student who played on the high school soccer team, I realized how hectic a schedule can get. Every day during the season, I had to go to practice after school from 3 PM to 5 PM. On game days, we had to leave right after school and usually arrived home at 9 PM on school nights. Many of my Saturdays were also dedicated to soccer games and practices.

Because of school athletics in America, students like me lost a lot of time and focus on school works. For the extremely talented high school athletes, high school sports allow them to gain a lot of confidence and drive them to work very hard on a sport for opportunities to play professionally. This confidence usually allows some of those students to abandon their school works and academic pursuits.

For me, I was never a good athlete or a great soccer player. Even with a mentality of participation, I got sidetracked from my educational priorities because of the hectic schedule during the soccer season. Of course, as a traditional Chinese boy, I continued to try my hardest to maintain my school achievements. Luckily I was able to fulfill the requirements of school classes in order to maintain quite solid grades. However, that was it. During the season, I could not really go beyond school requirements and continue to prepare myself further academically for my future. I could not even have extra time for personal reading and studying.

In addition to high school athletics, American high schools also offer many student-based clubs and organizations. Even at an average high school such as mine, there are plenty of student activities through the student clubs and organizations. At my high school, we have Student Council, Future Business Leaders of America, Academic Superbowl teams, DECA, Boys Legion, Girls League, Diversity Group, Challenge Day team, speech and debate team, etc. When I first moved to United States as a freshman in high school, my goal was to have a very American experience in a very American community. As a matter of fact, the community I moved to used to be the headquarter for the Ku Klux Klan, the anti-foreigner and pro-racism society! Because of my inherent goal, I joined many of the clubs and learned a lot about why American students don't put a lot of dedication to school works and education.

Since my arrival, I joined Student Council, Future Business Leaders of America, DECA, Boys Legion, Debate team, Academic Superbowl team, French Club, School Newspaper, and many more organizations. Of course, I placed my focus only on a few of the clubs I listed. But I joined all those clubs to meet people and to really get into the mentalities and lives of American high school students.

Like me, I found that many American students join more than one student organization. Because of this, they have to set aside a lot of time for each of those clubs. For example, Student Council always required mandatory community service activities and school service activities. Those activities require hours of planning and execution. I know because I was both a member and an officer.

Debate team is another example. Since my freshman year, I always wanted to challenge myself and jump out of my comfort zone. Since I always feared public speaking, especially since my first language was Chinese and I was inherently very shy, I became a dedicated member of the debate team. As an active member, I had to research debate topics and evidence throughout the week and to write many different debate cases. On Fridays, I had to practice countless hours and revise my debate cases. On Saturdays, I as a debate team member had to go to tournaments and compete in them. We usually left at 5 AM on Saturdays and come home at 6 PM. Because of all the hours I put into debate, I sometimes had to give up my academic and school work dedications.

In similar manner, Future Business Leaders of America takes me away from home on a regular basis to attend business conferences, meetings, workshops, and seminars. Additionally, FBLA also requires community service and club activities. As I approached my years as an upperclassman, I also took over leadership roles for the FBLA organization both in my school and in the state. In addition to my engagements and duties as a member such as service activities, I had to load more responsibilities on my back as a leader. This is the same for many of my American friends who also have to load up leadership roles for different clubs at school. More times are consumed through this opportunity.

All those opportunities I have through school clubs and organizations have dramatically decreased my focus and dedication on studying. These same opportunities have also inflicted all the American high school students as well. Not only did I lose time for school works and in-depth academic pursuits, I also realized that there is more to life than education. Because of such mentality, both young Americans and I lost our dedications to academic studies and unknowingly fell behind to the children on the other side of the globe who have no options other than school and tutoring.

Of course, one can argue that extracurricular activities and more opportunities in America are actually preparing young Americans for global competition. And I have to agree. They do better prepare young Americans for the real world and global competition. However, the only beneficiaries to those activities are young Americans who already succeed academically primarily. Education and school works are the primary determinants on a person's future success. And yet many still don't realize it in America.

Before a student can utilize the experience earned through all those activities, he or she needs to succeed in academia. Education is the primary obstacle. It's only through academic success he or she can attend university and attain a special career skill. It's through career skills a young American can join the global competition. With those career skills, young Americans can then use the leadership and service experiences in school activities to further themselves in their careers and gain an edge over young people from other countries. That would be great!

However, the problem that exists today is that many young Americans put too much focus on external opportunities in school and in community and fails to succeed academically. In some ways, those young people think one step ahead before passing the first obstacle called education. Sometimes, their excess focus on those options in life results in them tripping before those skills can be useful.

FIFTEEN

A Drive to Change Future

What is a driver's license? To many American young people, the answer is very simple. A driver's license is a photo ID that allows one to legally drive a car anywhere on land. Yet to many Chinese young people today, the answer is still quite a mystery. One of many reasons is that young Chinese don't have driver's licenses and young Americans do.

A driver's license may be just a little card that authorizes one to operate a vehicle. However, it carries significant ramifications. One of such ramification is the effect on the education and work ethics of students. Students are the future of nations, and they are no different in America and in China. That's why the educational path and work ethics they attain when young can be the determinant for the future outlook for a country in global competition.

In the status quo, the situation looks quite optimistic for the Chinese and somewhat pessimistic for the Americans. For some reasons, the Chinese students are getting stronger and more competitive while American students are standing still and more lackluster. A piece of the puzzle to this reality maybe something as little yet as powerful as a driver's license.

A small piece of object like a driver's license has affected American students for a long period of time. At the young age of 16, most American students have the privileges to attain a driver's license and operate a vehicle. The problem today does not reside with the object called driver's license. The problems rest on the powers the driver's license hold. Those powers are simply too great that not yet matured minds can allow them to be destructive and dangerous—not just physically.

As many of you may understand, attaining a driver's license is a great deal in a young person's life in United States. A driver's license carries symbolism in the lives of young Americans. With a driver's license, young Americans are not bond to the disciplines of the parents any longer. A driver's license advocates freedom in a young person's life. Prior to attaining driver's license, young Americans are bond to the control of the parents. They do not have the ability to escape from the disciplines of the parents. If a student were to rebel against the parents, he or she really has no place to go. He or she is bond to the local community within walking distances. Such limitation and inability to escape can be quite discouraging for young Americans. That's why young Americans prior to the age of 16 are usually more disciplined and more controlled.

At the age of 16, the driver's license changes the arrangement of control completely. Originally, the parents could have control over the children because the children are bond to the local community within walking distance. With driver's license, the bond disappears. Because a driver's license allows young people to operate cars, many young Americans can regain control to their lives at an early age. If their parents were to discipline the children, the children can actually rebel and ran away with the car. In many ways, the driver's license redistributes the power of the family and gives the young ones the options to be less disciplined and more disobedient.

As we all know quite clearly, young people like me make a lot of vacuous and uncalled for mistakes. Our immaturity and lack of experience in life allow us to lose self-control on many occasions in our young lives. Because of the lack of inhibition and self-control, the car can be very dangerous in our hands. Since the parents lose control of us when we attain the driver's license and a car, we usually are able to do what we want and get away with it.

I have American friends who attained driver's license and cars when they turned 16. With their cars, they often disregard their school works and future ambitions. Sometimes, my friends sneak out in the middle of a school night and go catch a movie. Later, they may go hang out and stay up for the entire night. Such actions are detrimental to their education at school. They usually sleep in class. They always purposely forget to do homework. Sometimes, they also forget to prepare for tests and assessments because they were able to escape from home at night with their cars and to party all night long.

One of such friends is my friend Jason. We were not only classmates, but we were also great friends in high school. I have known him since my freshman year when I first moved to United States. Honestly, I admired him very much. I can remember him to be very well spoken and very intelligent. Not only did he do well in class, he had great aspirations for life. I can recall that he always wanted to become a lawyer when he grows up. In addition to his academic achievements at school during my freshman year, he was also well-rounded. He was an important member of the school debate team and an active player for my high school's football team. In many ways, he was this All-American boy with a very promising future ahead of him.

Unfortunately, this image of him in my mind quickly changed as we went into our sophomore year. Because he had an early birthday, he attained his driver's license in the beginning of his sophomore year. With a driver's license, his behaviors became more eccentric and more rebellious. Through my eyes, I realized that he changed for the worse with his driver's license. His original dedications to school and to his future faded away as he appeared to gain too much control over his life due to the driver's license.

In class, he, on numerous occasions, suggested to skip school after lunch. Since we often had one period of class after lunch, he often skipped that period of class. Before long weekends or long breaks, he often missed classes on the last day of school. Even when he was in class, he was a different person compared to him during his freshman year. He was no longer attentive. Because he could drive, he always liked to go out on school nights and return late at night. As a result, he had to sleep in class on multiple occasions, which directly affected his education and future. Sometimes, I feel bad for him because his driver's license and his car had taken over his life.

Going out at night can seem quite harmless sometimes. However, its ramifications are dangerous to the education and work ethics of young Americans. Having a car and a driver's license can promote skipping school like my friend Jason did. I have seen new high school drivers developing into two groups of people at my school. On one hand, I have peers and friends who would skip a period of class (usually the last period) and go to a restaurant or someone's house during school day. They were good kids when they were freshmen in high school. But because of attaining driver's license in their sophomore year, they then had the opportunity and the ability to skip a period of class.

In the end, two results usually happen. First, they can get caught by the school and end up being suspended. Second, they can miss a period of an important class with unexcused absence and get docked on their grades at school. Neither result is great for their future and their educational path.

On the other hand, there are students at my school who would skip an entire day of school and drive to some other cities for fun with their friends. Sure, it's fun! I want to do it sometimes too! Their immaturity makes them ignorant of the consequences.

First and foremost, those students would get disciplined by the school in the future. Secondly, their school works and educational endeavors are completely ruined with a day or two of unexcused absences. Most importantly, having the option to drive a car and skip school affects the work ethics and dedications of many young Americans. To be honest, skipping school by itself really does not have major long-term consequences in a young person's life. However, this option does reshape the work ethics and lazy habits of these young people's lives. These young people are going to face competitions from China and India where students have dedicated hours and days continuously on education and future career. This type of competition can be quite lopsided if young Americans adapt to such lazy and ignorant habits and work ethics.

One word that I have mentioned in this chapter and in this book repeatedly is the word "option". In another chapter, I have already discussed the consequences of options on American young people. In this circumstance, the driver's license provides young people with more options in life. Yes, options are good. Options represent opportunities and the foundation of United States. However, options are dangerous for young people.

Because of options provided by the driver's license, young Americans can then take advantage of the options and make some very bad choices. In many cases, it's not their faults. Their minds are naturally undeveloped and less mature. I can understand this because I am a teenager myself. With options, our immature minds and little life experiences can be very dangerous.

This reality is similar to fire and oxygen. Both are great. Fire provides heat, and oxygen provides air for us to breath. However, the mixture and fire and oxygen are dangerous and detrimental. Similarly, young Americans are great, and options are wonderful. However, the combination of the two can be dangerous as well. I don't want to single out young Americans. If Chinese young people are offered with similar options such as driver's license, the result would be the same. But fortunately for the Chinese society, the Chinese young people don't really have those options.

One reason that Chinese young people are not really affected by the driver's license and its great powers is that they mostly don't have driver's license. There are two obstacles for Chinese teenagers before driving. In the first place, the legal driving age in China is 18 years old instead of 16 years old. Maybe you think that the two-year difference is not significant. Yet it is. For young Americans, they usually attain their driver's licenses as early as the beginning of their sophomore year in high school. In other words, the driver's license is going to affect the remaining three years of high school for those students. This is very detrimental to the development of young Americans because high school is usually the place to shape individuals. The ones who succeed in high school get to attend college and inch closer to a career later in life. Those who fail in high school are not able to attend higher education institutions. This will most definitely place them as the lost causes. They are the ones who struggle from living day to day. Because high school is so important, driving age of 16 instead of 18 makes a great difference.

In China, the minimum driving age of 18 limits Chinese young people to drive after high school only. Since the age of entering school in China is a little younger than that of America, almost all Chinese students who are eligible to drive already finished high school. Luckily for them, the time when they can attain a driver's license is a time after they have already been molded as individuals. It's also the age when many Chinese students have already determined whether they will continue with higher education.

Unlike the United States, the minimum driving age is really not the major limitation to young people driving in China. The major obstacle for them is purchasing a vehicle. In the United States, average young people usually attain a car in two ways. For one, they can take an old car passed down from a family member. Or they can also purchase a second-hand car with as low a price as $1000. Young Americans are very fortunate in this respect, and the Chinese young people are not so lucky. In China, most adults cannot even afford cars. In America, a person's annual salary can pretty much guarantee the abilities to buy a car. In China, however, it takes years of saving to buy a car for a white-collar professional. Even if he or she buys a car, he or she still has to deal with the high costs of gasoline in China.

As we can see, even adults in China struggle with buying a car. There is almost no chance for an average Chinese teenager at the age of 18 to have a car to drive. The costs of the cars and gasoline are simply too high—even in today's China. Cars in China are delicacies. They are usually the properties of the wealthy. In the United States, however, having a car is as common as a Chinese owning a bicycle. That's how commonplace cars are to average Americans.

Of course, a lack of cars has been a benefit to the progress and competitive nature of the Chinese society. While almost all Chinese young people are missing out on the opportunities to operate a vehicle, they also avoided great seductions to their work ethics and school achievements. They do not have luxuries to skip school in the middle of the day or at the middle of the night. If they do want to commit such actions, they have to use bikes, their legs, or a city bus. All those options are too inconvenient. Therefore, many of those ideas and actions are free from the minds of many young Chinese today.

The lack of the driving option has prevented Chinese young people from getting sidetracked and enabled them to work harder toward their education and career goals. This same type of dedication has also made them extremely competitive and intimidating on the international stage.

So now many Americans have awakened from the reality of international competition. And many parents, students, and professionals in America are trying to find answers to correctly deal with those competitions. From my experience here, I learned that many Americans today are looking at the most conspicuous and most direct reasons to the quick rise of the Chinese such as the education system and policies. Yes, they are very important in shaping the young people of China.

However, it's also time to see what Americans have been doing wrong on every day issues.

Although difference on education system and policies is a major contributor to today's reality, there are many little reasons on the habits of young Americans that have caused such decline in American education system. One of those little reasons is driving in high school. When I discussed this reason to my friends and my parents, they think I am crazy in believing that driving at an early age of 16 has affected the educational excellence in America. Even my mother thinks this reason is silly. But I am sure that they are wrong.

In life, it's always the little things that lead to great problems. In this case, the little thing is driving. While driving in high school seems both negligent and inconsequential to the development of young Americans in education and in their career futures, it does carry great impacts. If driving had not lead young Americans to skipping school and losing time on academic studying, many young Americans today including several of my friends would most likely to continue working hard at school and to become valuable members of the society. In China, students do not make it in life and in education because the competitions are too stiff and personal abilities are somewhat limited.

If this were true in America, I would never write this book. The reason I am writing this book because I found that many talented young Americans do not succeed at school and later in their careers. It's not because they don't have enough talents or abilities to face competitions. It's because of little distractions such as driving that prevent them from focusing on education and on future success. This has been really detrimental to Americans in dealing with global competition.

A famous philosopher and writer Goethe once said, "The hardest thing to see is what is in front of your eyes." He was 100% correct. In our circumstance today, driving in high school is something obvious. It's right in front of our eyes. However, it has been very difficult for us to see its effects on the development of young Americans. Hopefully, this reality can quickly change.

SIXTEEN

Controlling vs. Cool Parents

Remember the classic TV show *Tom and Jerry*? If you don't know or don't remember, *Tom and Jerry* was a world-wide renowned cartoon that had won seven Academy Awards. It was about a cat and a mouse. Tom, the cat, always wanted to chase and capture the mouse Jerry. In order to accomplish his plan, Tom constantly placed traps for Jerry to fall into. Because Tom continuously and unyieldingly tested Jerry, Jerry became smarter and smarter. In return, the mouse Jerry always tried to outsmart Tom. As a result, Jerry always succeeded. This cartoon represents a classic case of one person inspiring another to be better through constant tests and challenges.

In reality, this type of relationship occurs in both sports and real life. In sports, we can always see the dominant athletes such as Roger Federer (Tennis), Tiger Woods (Golf), and Kobe Bryant (Basketball) act as motivations to inspire younger but emerging athletes like Rafael Nadal (Tennis), Anthony Kim (Golf), and Lebron James (Basketball). In real life, the Chinese parents practice the same ideology. They understand that the only way for their children to succeed in education and to prepare for global competition is through constant parental discipline, pressure, and challenge. On the contrary, American parents do not. This reality has created a disparity between Chinese young people and American young people today.

In China, the parents are more strict and forceful, especially on the topic of education. I am sure that this fact does not surprise anyone in America. Ever since I moved to America, this is the one singled out reason I have heard from Americans on Chinese young people's success with education. Although I affirm this perception, there are more depths and complexities to this idea.

One reason that Chinese parents are hard on their children in relation to education is family rivalry. This is quite uncommon in America. American parents, on most occasions, allow their children to follow their own paths and try to give them more space. They most often advocate more independence for their children. Of course, I am sure that some American parents have used their children as tools for personal rivalry on certain occasions, but the Chinese parents have raised the rivalry to a new level. Sometimes, I feel that their children and their successes have evolved as the most important topic of discussion among Chinese families.

Among the Chinese parents, there will always be discussions on the success of their children. While Americans may like to brag about their new house on the beach or new Cadillac, Chinese like to show off their children. Through those discussions and competitions, the Chinese parents would most likely to find some weaknesses in their children compared to the children of their friends. It's either their grades at school or their inability to win major competitions. By learning these weaknesses in comparison, the Chinese parents would always go home and push their children harder. By doing so, they accomplish two tasks. First, they have protected their personal prides facing their friends. Second, they challenged their children and allowed them to be more humble and successful in education and future career.

Even though I appreciate the effects of competition and rivalries between Chinese families, I personally detest it in real life through my own experiences. My mother is very image conscious. She always wants to look good and successful in front of her friends like many Chinese families in the community. Because of such state of mind, she always wants me to be more successful in school in order to protect her image both as an individual and as s parent. I personally think this is quite selfish. But what can I do when every Chinese parent is doing the same thing. And somehow it has worked for them in raising a group of very fine young people who are quite prepared for globalization.

I can still remember picnics hosted by local Chinese communities. This is a gathering where all Chinese families from the area come together and have a "fun" day. During these gatherings, the Chinese families always like to bring their trophy sons and daughters. Unlike American gatherings where people talk about vacations and sports, these gatherings consist of parents talking about their children and their accomplishments at school. Almost every time, they treat these conversations and events as competitions to advance family rivalry. They want to know who raised a better son or daughter. Since I am an average Chinese teenager without some extraordinary accomplishments, I would never hear the end of my mother's stories about her friends' sons and daughters.

“Did you know that Huang just came back from a university after conducting several researches on cancer? What did you do, Xiuzhe?”

“Did you hear that Wang just come back from Yale for the summer and is working as an intern for a Fortune 500 company? I wish I have a kid like that.”

“Are you aware that Yang just scored a perfect on the SAT and the ACT? You have so much more work to do. Why can’t I have a son like that?”

I always hear those comments from my mother after she talked to their so-called friends during those picnics. My mother is very competitive, and she always wants to feel superior compared to other parents. Likewise, other Chinese parents do the same in return. That’s why they constantly compare the accomplishments of their children. Usually, I get the short-end of the stick, and my mother always uses other people’s success as motivation for me to work even harder.

Without a doubt, the tactic worked. However, I feel exhausted personally. Sometimes, I also feel that my mother is not proud of my accomplishments, no matter how little they are. This feeling is inherited by many of my Chinese brothers and sisters (not siblings but all Chinese young people). Despite the positive effects of competition and personal pride of the parents, their posterities are usually hurt through declining confidence and morality. In return, low confidence and morality frequently make Chinese young people like me to be more inclined to work harder on education and preparation for the future.

Besides the comparisons, Chinese parents differ from American parents in another fashion. As we all know, Americans are very positive people. I have been around parents of my American friends long enough to know how they educate their children. One conspicuous aspect of American parenting style is encouragement. American parents like to encourage and praise children on every little accomplishment. Although this is not true for every American parent, this is generally true as we speak.

When a child earns an A at school, the American parents would usually praise the child and tell him or her how proud they are with the grades. Such action occurs repeatedly throughout a child's life in United States through my observation. Even when a C student comes home with a B-, the American parents sometimes will celebrate for the improvement. Additionally, American parents like to tell their children that they can do anything if they set their minds on it. They like to make their children think that everything is possible.

Though praises and encouragements are good, they can be somewhat detrimental as well. Because American children think that they are extremely good at everything due to parents' encouragements, they tend to be overconfident. Overconfidence then leads to lack of efforts in different aspects of life such as education.

For example, one of my American friends always gets A's at school. As a result, her parents always praise her achievements and grades. She always gets good allowances and amazing gifts when she receives those grades. Such encouragements give her great satisfactions and make her think that she does not have to work hard at school any more. This type of overconfidence constraints her potential from pursuing more challenging academic works. If she were to combine her innate abilities with more dedication without feeling overconfident, I would never be surprised when she wins a Nobel Prize in science or mathematics.

On the opposite of this spectrum, there are Chinese parents. Chinese parents, in general, tend to use a very different parenting tactic. Instead of giving praise and encouragement following triumphs, Chinese parents always like to find mistakes in those triumphs and identify areas for improvement. They believe that humbleness and modesty are the best ways to maintain current success and reach greater triumphs later.

This is exactly how my parents educate me throughout my life. When I received A's on my report cards from school, my parents, especially my mother, always ask me why I could not have more A+'s instead of A's. When I received a very solid score for my SAT test, my parents always scolded me for not receiving a higher grade like 2400. When I received a 4 on my AP English test, my parents confronted me and interrogated me on why I could not receive a 5. When I got elected as the State Vice-President of a student business organization, my parents questioned me and asked why I could not become president. Those are some examples of their tactics.

Chinese parents like to encourage dissatisfactions among their children. This way, the children like I would not be satisfied and would continue to work for something better. Such parenting style usually results in higher achievements among Chinese students. As an observer, I would probably think that such tactic is absolutely brilliant. It truly is a great way to motivate and challenge human mentality. However, from personal experience, I don't really like it when my parents ask for more when I already did pretty well! Yet the tactic has worked, and I am happy to see myself improve everyday instead of standing still.

In addition to competition among parents, the transitional period of time in China at the present moment also affects the parents' way of educating their children. Nowadays, we are witnessing a transitional period in China as it shifts and transforms from the old to the new. The Chinese parents and children today are called the transitional generations.

This unique condition has created two distinctive group of people—the parents and the children. The parents represent the old generation in China. Since they lived through a period of tough times in Chinese history, they have experienced ample disappointments. They never enjoyed the opportunities that exist today with new Chinese capitalism and globalization. Because they have many disappointments as the old end of the transitional stick, they have many hopes and aspirations unfulfilled. This is where the discipline and pressure on education come in. The disappointments and unfulfilled dreams are usually passed onto the succeeding generation. The Chinese parents want their children to finally accomplish those dreams such as high-level of education, career success, and prominent status in society. That's why they push their children to the limit in education. That's also why they tend to over prepare their successors for the global competition.

Many may argue that American parents do the same because they have unfulfilled dreams as well. While this may be true to some extent, American parents are nowhere close to Chinese parents on past disappointments. In the first place, our time is not a transitional period in American history. Since America has been a world power for many years, it already has several generations of success. Correspondingly, a lot more American parents and adults have fulfilled their dreams through existing opportunities. Conversely, Chinese parents never enjoyed the same opportunities. Because of more fulfillments throughout their lives, parents in America do not push children as hard on education and career success.

At the same time, the mentalities are fundamentally different between American and Chinese parents. American parents are more liberal in educating children compared to their counterparts in China. I personally feel that they are more lax and mellow. Through my American friends, I learned that traditional American parents want their children to find their own ways—no matter how wealthy the family is.

In general, they prefer the Laissez-faire policy toward their children instead of the totalitarian policy like common Chinese parents. This policy may be a reflection of the American national ideals, government policies, and economic policies. In accordance to Laissez-faire parenting methods, American parents give their children opportunities to make mistakes and to explore with their own decision makings. Instead of constantly pressuring the children to study and to focus on education, they actually allow their children to follow their own interests. Although this is not true for every American family, this is a general trend that I see in America. People can argue against this point of view, but there are definitely certain amounts of truth to this perception on American parents.

Simultaneously, another factor that has affected the Chinese parenting style is social and retirement security. Like many developing countries, China has never been and does not have a stable retirement policy. In the past few years, Chinese government has done a lot to secure retirement benefits for all public employees. However, the mentality for lack of retirement benefits has well been established among Chinese parents and adults today. Through past instabilities in this area and established beliefs, Chinese parents usually invest their retirement future on their child.

If their child were to be successful in education and in his or her career, he or she can later have enough funds to take care of the parents during retirement. Nowadays, this investment is very risky for Chinese parents. They only have one opportunity for it to yield high returns! The One-Child Policy only allows Chinese parents to have one child, and it has added a lot of pressure on Chinese parents.

The pressures on Chinese parents have been transferred from the parents to the children. In order to secure their retirement future, Chinese parents need to raise a potentially successful child who would earn enough money to take care of the parents. In China today, the safest and most reliable way to success is through education. That's why Chinese parents are hard on their children when it comes to school works and grades.

If any person were to understand the role of retirement future on parents and their children, this person would most definitely be me. Throughout my 17 years of life with my parents, I have always been burdened with my parents' future. My mother always reminds me that her hard works and expenditures on me are investments. I need to repay her by taking care of her when she becomes old.

This has been a component of Chinese tradition and culture for a long period of time. This is also a demonstration of respect in my culture. While I have accepted the idea of taking care of my parents after retirement, I cannot stand the fact that they tell me this all the time. Sometimes, my mother even likes to guilt me with this idea. She always tells me that she doesn't want her investments in me to become wastes. I was pressured to work harder in school in order to have abilities to take care of her later in life.

Sometimes, I feel that American children are lucky. They have more freedoms and more opportunities to choose their own life. In some ways, I feel that my life path has already been chosen for me. While this is a very sad reality for me, I understand that there are millions of Chinese teenagers who are facing more difficult pressures from their parents. While the success of young Chinese people in education and careers is not an accident, it's not an easy position to be in either.

With an amalgamation of interfamily competition, personal pride, transitional pressure, and unsecured retirement, Chinese parents have become the guardians to their children's future. As guardians, they can adopt totalitarian rule within the family unlike many American families. This combination has been mixed and intensified with the social fabric of China.

In the Chinese society, the parents have a firm belief that the respects of their children are automatic. This is quite different from America. In America, many parents believe that the respects are earned instead of given automatically. Because of this disparity in belief and expectation, Chinese parents are more demanding of their children. American parents are trying to gain the respects of their children. Sometimes, their pursuits for respect prevent them from being too forceful with their children. They get too bogged down. Such pursuit results in American parents being friends to their children instead of disciplinarians.

On the contrary, Chinese parents already take respects for granted and demand more such as educational success. The social fabric of the Chinese society has already given Chinese parents many fiated powers and allow them to have more time to demand more on the educational front. This condition directly place Chinese parents into the driver seat as disciplinarians to their children instead of their friends.

Furthermore, Chinese parents have more control over their children than American parent do. American parents use the Laissez-faire parenting style as I mentioned earlier. This style usually makes American young people more independent at a young age. Today, middle school and high school American students have jobs. Jobs not only distribute more power to young Americans, but also give them enough strength to act as mavericks.

If American parents were to demand more educational success, their children can disregard this demand because they have jobs and do not necessarily need total financial supports from the parents. This gives teenagers both mental and financial boosts facing their parents.

In the meantime, there is a very different story for young Chinese. Traditionally, Chinese teenagers do not have opportunities to work at a young age like their American counterparts. Even if they do have opportunities, most Chinese parents would shut the idea down from the beginning and demand more time to be used on education. This makes young Chinese more dependent upon their parents.

Dependencies always result in more power given to the Chinese parents. If I, as a Chinese teen without a job, were to disobey the wishes of my parents, they would always threaten me with no further financial support. Sometimes, this reality makes me feel like a bird without wings. I cannot fly out of the nest and the parents as eagles constantly control my actions due to my inability to fly.

In essence, societal disparity and the distinctive social fabric of each society have distinguished the effects of parents on children. American parents, in general, place less pressure and allow more independence for their children. As a result, the minds and judgments of young people take over as the driver in their lives. While this is great for naturally ambitious young people, this has many risks because many young people can run into accidents.

Meanwhile, Chinese parents remain as the drivers to the lives of young people in China. Of course, such limits from the parents hinder naturally ambitious young people from growing at a swift rate. Nevertheless, this same control from the parents is a safer policy and allows more Chinese young people to succeed without any accidents or mishaps in the middle.

SEVENTEEN

Now what?

In the previous chapters, we have seen the factors that have contributed to the disparity between young people in China and in America. Of course, if you have been paying attention, you probably have realized that my observations and experiences have shown young Americans in a disadvantaged position in global competition. I have discussed the dedications and hard works Chinese young people put into their education. Through their education and academic success, many of them have gained valuable career skills and intellectual knowledge at very young ages. As a result, they become more prepared on the international stage facing global competition.

With this reality in mind, many of you probably become more anxious and fearful about the future ahead for the young Americans. For many of you, America's place on the world stage in the future is still very uncertain as China threatens to take over the prominent position. So what can we do as Americans to deal with this dilemma? Should we just give up? Or should we find ways to combat this disadvantaged position?

I suggest the latter as the solution. Personally, I have always been a huge fan of the American style of education. If this were not the case, I would never have moved to United States with my parents. For many years when I was living in China, my parents had been working countless hours to make immigration to North America a possibility. That's how bad we wanted to come to America and experience the opportunities and options we would never hope to have in China.

It's quite a pity that young Americans today have taken those opportunities and options to an extreme. Instead of using them as a pad launching them into the world as prepared and successful adults, they have been taking advantage of them and use them as disadvantages and distractions preventing them from creating a successful future. Sometimes, I cannot even bear to think about those wasted opportunities.

As always, we cannot change the past. We cannot change the realities that have already happened today to young Americans like my friends I mentioned in previous chapters. They have all been intoxicated by the unlimited freedoms and options within this great nation. All we can do is look at the future and decide whether we want to change today's unfortunate reality. The good news is that intoxication is not permanent, and there is always time when we can wake up from a bad hangover. And this time is now, my friends.

As I observe instances when young Americans throw their future and competitive edge away, I can always see blinks of lights. When I witness the greatness of this nation and its ideals, I can never doubt any chances for Americans, both young and old, to make a U-turn on this erroneous path. As a young man who lived in both North America and Asia, I see unique opportunities for Americans to get back in the game and become once again dominant players in global competition.

Today, we are witnessing two extremes in shaping the lives of young people through education. On one hand, we see the Chinese society that offers its young people no freedom or options whatsoever. The parents in this society push their children to the extreme on discipline and dedication to education. Sometimes, students even detest learning because of the extreme style of teaching and educating. In this environment, the education path is very rigid and inflexible. It's almost like a factory assembly line. The young people go through this system like robots because they can only follow instructions. In the end, majority of Chinese young people successfully complete their education path and acquires sufficient knowledge and wisdom academically for global competition.

On the other hand, we see another extreme on the opposite end in America. In this half of the world, the society promotes freedom of choice for its young people. While parents are still the disciplinarians of households and teachers are still in charge of the students at school, the young people are ultimately the drivers for their lives. There are a lot of options and opportunities in America. Many times, the adults allow young people to choose their own paths in life and in education.

Unlike the rigid and factory-like environment in China, America is more like a theme park with different rides. Because there is no specific route for the young people, they can choose any rides in this theme park. Sometimes, this is quite dangerous. Because of lack of rigidity, many young people in America can sometimes get too preoccupied with a ride or two and drop out of the route. In this case, they do not complete their education and are not prepared for tomorrow's global competition. The success rate of this system is quite low because not many young people can finish the path.

Through both my observation and the assertions of many pundits, we have seen two different patterns in the two societies. In China, the education system and the values of the majority have limited young people from truly unleashing their full potentials. In such a system, the ones with great self-control and ambitions cannot really achieve to their full abilities and potentials. Such young people who can balance education with extracurricular activities cannot excel under restrictions of the parents and the society.

Likewise, the ones with less self-restrain and ambitions have to follow the rigid path of education and usually succeed by becoming useful members of society who can compete for jobs globally. Although they were not supposed to succeed under a freer environment, the enforcements and tough disciplines of the society have prevented them from failing. As a result of such rigid system, majority of young people in China become educated and skilled in a career field. They usually end up being quite competitive in global competition.

However, there is a gigantic downside to the Chinese system. For a long time, China has been using this system to create ample educated and able young people. As a matter of fact, this system has a very high success rate because of its rigid standards and restrictions. Almost all Chinese young people who went through this system become quite educated academically and skilled in different career fields. Yet today, America still has the greatest economy in the world, no matter how bad the recession is. The most brilliant minds and individuals such as Bill Gates and Warren Buffets are all from America. But why?

Through the Chinese system, there are many averagely good individuals, but there are almost no great individuals. A great example would be the statistics to Nobel Prize winners. United States alone, not to mention other western nations, has over 200 Nobel Prize winners in different categories such as physics, chemistry, economics, and peace. In contrast, China, a country that puts heavy emphasis on education and young people development, has none. This example alone shows us that the Chinese system is only good at shaping many individuals who will become successful members of the world community, but they are not likely to be the best. America, on the contrary, produces the best and the brightest individuals who will excel in global competition.

To me, this reality is not very surprising. Ever since I moved to America, I realized that it is a great place to raise and develop the most exceptional and brightest individuals. Under a more liberal and freer environment, young people who truly are ambitious can actually excel. Not only will they continue to strive for academic achievements, these students at young ages have the opportunities to polish their leadership skills, their communication skills, their social skills, their experimental skills, and many more. Those are something extremely ambitious and intelligent young people in China cannot do. As a result, these American young people get the best of both worlds through a balanced lifestyle and truly become the best in the world. In contrast, the Chinese system has created an equal distribution system in which the less motivated does not get left behind, and the more motivated do not excel due to restraints.

Because of the condition mentioned above, I am absolutely sure that young Americans today can jump back into the game. They can become really competitive facing international competitions if they change their mentalities and work ethics. As a solution, the American education system and the American society itself need to create a new balance that still does not exist in today's America and China.

Today, China and America are both going into the extremes. China is very conservative in regard to educating young people. Young Chinese do not have the opportunities to truly unleash their full potentials. They are not developing in a well-rounded manner. Because the Chinese society badly wants the young people to succeed, its system of education for young people are too rigid and too systematic. In return, those young people cannot become the best in the world.

America, however, offers too much liberalism and freedom in education. There are too many options, and many young people cannot make it in the end because of those options and freedom. Only those who create a balance between education and extracurricular activities succeed and become the best. However, the percentage of those young people is too small, and too many young people have thrown away their lives at a young age.

The greatest problem in America today is the success rate of educating young people. The outright freedoms for young people have been detrimental to America's future. While freedom is good in moderation, today's excess in freedom for young Americans has severely lowered the success rate of converting children into successful and competitive adults. Sure, the best and the brightest in the world are still Americans. However, this group of people is simply too small, and America cannot afford to leave so many young people behind.

That's why we need balance in America. Everything in life is the best with moderation. For young Americans to succeed with globalization in the future, this new balance is vital. Instead of offering excess freedoms to young Americans, American education system, educators, and parents should usher in a new age of discipline and control.

Of course, we do not want to see America as a counterpart of China. I am not suggesting that Americans should take away all the freedoms and options. That would be foolish and unfavorable. I do suggest that there should be a balance between freedom and restrictions. To take the first step, parents today have to reshape their roles and their responsibilities.

Nowadays, American parents mostly have been playing passive roles in the lives of their children. This is especially true when we compare American parents with the Chinese parents. In order to create this necessary balance, the parents need to take an active role. They need to place more attentions on all their children. When young Americans are distracted and sidetracked, American parents need to correct it immediately. Of course, I do not want to see American parents to become those overbearing Chinese parents. However, their roles need to increase and to be stricter. For example, excessive free time should be limited, and personal distractions such as iPods and gaming systems should be limited.

In similar manner, the American education system needs to be revamped. Through my experience in this system, I have found many flaws. In some ways, the education system has placed the young people in a disadvantaged position. First and foremost, there is simply too much toleration in the American education system with inappropriate behaviors. Such toleration has allowed distracting behaviors and actions to thrive in the education system.

Additionally, the curriculum of the education system is too simple, especially in high schools. It's not sufficient enough for young Americans to face and challenge their counterparts in China. This not-so-rigorous curriculum is especially true in the public education system. On many occasions, I have found the excuse educators have made to be ridiculous. Many of them believe that "there are still many students in the system who cannot deal with a more rigorous curriculum, and the system does not want to leave them behind." The excuse itself is a great flaw. The current American education system does not hold young people and their parents accountable for challenging academic work. If the system were to raise the level of academic curriculum since first grade, the students would most likely become adapt to such curriculum and challenge themselves more.

Last but not least, young Americans themselves are responsible to make changes in order to adapt for global competition. While parents and the education system are very influential to today's reality, the students themselves need to change their mentalities. In my opinion, young Americans today need to see from an international perspective instead of a local perspective. This is necessary as their competitors due to globalization are no longer just people around them. They are now from all countries in the world such as China. With this new perspective, young Americans need to rethink about what's necessary to succeed and to be competitive. They can no longer play and relax all day. They cannot just fulfill the standards of American education system. Young Americans, from their new global perspective, need to put more dedication and investments into their future. This includes more self-restrain and more ambitions.

Today, the only path to redemption and to change in America is unity and synergy. It's no longer a mystery that China and India are rising at an exponential rate with their group of driven young people. Nowadays, American society in general, the education system, educators, parents, and young people need to work together in order to keep pace with the surge from other nations. Every group mentioned needs to make necessary changes, both physically and mentally, to face globalization and a new wave of global competition. If one group fails to make necessary reforms, the entire system will falter. That's how important and critical unity and synergy is today.

Among us, there will always be naysayers and skeptics. They will probably say, "We don't need any change. China has always produced a large group of young intellectuals who wanted to challenge us. After all these years, we are still the best in the world, and our people always end up being the best." Please do not get fooled by such rhetoric. Today, we are facing a whole new ball game.

Sure, China has been trying for years to become the strongest country in the world. And of course, that goal has not yet been fulfilled. However, Americans should not be deceived by the past resilience and use it as the fool's gold. As a Chinese insider, I have been following the Chinese educational policies very closely. Today, they have a new plan. Unlike many Americans today, the Chinese has realized their short-comings in educating young people. They have realized that they have been too extreme with academic enforcements.

Nowadays, they are trying to incorporate a more western style of education into their traditional approach to education. They are not only aiming to create a large group of young people who are academically competent, but they are also trying to develop a more well-rounded group of young people. This is very scary. This new set of policy will not only strengthen the originally positive aspects of the Chinese system, but this will also take away the advantages American young people have had for years.

When I was in fourth grade, I had a great opportunity to run for the class president. Many people were supporting me, and I had great advantages to win. On the day before the election, two classmates, who hated me, came up and talked to me. They told me that I would never win the election. They told me that I had no chance. Because I listened to those naysayers, I decided not to run for president. Later, majority of my classmates went to talk to me and asked me why I didn't run. They told me that if I were to run, I would have become the class president. Since that day, I have been regretting that decision ever since. I still remember that day and blame myself for making a poor choice because of those two naysayers. I truly hope Americans like you will not make the same mistake as I did. Passing on opportunities and refusing to use reasons are the greatest tragedies in life. Those two may well be the downfalls of America in its defeat in global competition if Americans continue to listen to the naysayers. There is a fierce urgency in the air, and now the choice is yours.